THE
"I LOVE MY AIR FRYER"

Cooking for One

RECIPE BOOK

175 Easy and Delicious Single-Serving Recipes, from *Chicken Parmesan* to *Pineapple Upside-Down Cake* and More

Heather Johnson
of TheFoodHussy.com

Adams Media
New York   London   Toronto   Sydney   New Delhi

Thank you to Amy, who has been my best friend forever and is "home" to me.
To Jesse, the dogs, and the cats for loving me unconditionally.
And to Stephanie, who pushed me to succeed through her advice and friendship.

Adams Media
An Imprint of Simon & Schuster, Inc.
100 Technology Center Drive
Stoughton, Massachusetts 02072

First Adams Media trade paperback edition January 2023

ADAMS MEDIA and colophon are trademarks of Simon & Schuster.

For information about special discounts for bulk purchases, please contact Simon & Schuster Special Sales at 1-866-506-1949 or business@simonandschuster.com.

The Simon & Schuster Speakers Bureau can bring authors to your live event. For more information or to book an event contact the Simon & Schuster Speakers Bureau at 1-866-248-3049 or visit our website at www.simonspeakers.com.

Photographs by James Stefiuk

Manufactured in the United States of America

4 2024

Library of Congress Cataloging-in-Publication Data
Names: Johnson, Heather, 1973– author.
Title: The "I love my air fryer" cooking for one recipe book / Heather Johnson of TheFoodHussy.com.
Description: Stoughton, Massachusetts: Adams Media, [2023] | Series: "I love my" series | Includes index.
Identifiers: LCCN 2022035048 | ISBN 9781507220092 (pb) | ISBN 9781507220108 (ebook)
Subjects: LCSH: Hot air frying. | Cooking for one. | LCGFT: Cookbooks.
Classification: LCC TX689 .J64 2023 | DDC 641.7/7--dc23/eng/20220803
LC record available at https://lccn.loc.gov/2022035048

ISBN 978-1-5072-2009-2
ISBN 978-1-5072-2010-8 (ebook)

Contents

Introduction

Sometimes making a multiple-serving meal just doesn't make sense. You may live by yourself and find that the average recipe results in too many leftovers, or you may have a guest with dietary restrictions. Perhaps you want to try a new dish before serving it to your picky eaters, or you just need a small, sweet bite at the end of a long day. Whatever the reason, these air fryer cooking for one recipes make things simple and delicious.

Whether you're new to the air fryer or have been using one for years, this book is for you. You can use the air fryer to cook entrées, breakfasts, side dishes, desserts, and more. At its core, this popular, multifunctional machine acts as a small countertop convection oven that fries food with circulated air. Hot air circulates around the food, creating a crispy exterior around a juicy interior, all without excess oil and fat. It's faster than a traditional oven! This device also eliminates the need for a deep fryer, microwave, and dehydrator. You are not limited to traditional fried foods—it can bake or roast items too. Because it replaces so many other appliances, you can cut down on kitchen clutter.

In this book, you'll find 175 healthy and versatile air fryer recipes that combine delicious flavors with generous single-serving portions. Here you'll find delicious single-serving recipes for every meal of the day, ranging from Strawberry Scones for breakfast to Garlic Herb Artichoke Hearts as a side dish, Chicken Cordon Bleu or Caprese-Stuffed Chicken Breasts for dinner, and some sweet Air Fryer–Grilled Peaches for dessert. In addition to delicious recipes, this cookbook includes many suggestions for easy prep and seasoning substitutions to add flavor and convenience. This way, you can customize these recipes to best suit your needs. Throughout this book, you'll find tips on how to prepare a meal for one and how to properly care for your air fryer. You will even find a list of some helpful kitchen accessories.

You'll learn how to use these single-serving recipes to save on kitchen space, time, money, and solo trips to the drive-through. Get ready to personalize your menu; create filling, flavorful, and healthy meals; and cook for one. Let's get air frying!

Cooking for One with an Air Fryer

Air fryers have really risen in popularity in the last few years because of their short cooking times. Whether you are a seasoned air fryer chef or brand-new to the appliance, this chapter will provide you with the differences between air fryer types, tips on cleaning your fryer, and a short list of useful tools and ingredients. While air fryers vary in size, shape, and functionality, the basic cooking technology is the same in each version. Read through your air fryer's manual and wash all removable parts with warm, soapy water before cooking your first meal.

Why Air Frying?

Air frying is becoming popular worldwide because you can cook foods quickly, easily, and with less oil, eliminating a lot of the health risks of frying.

Here are a few other reasons to explore air frying:

- Your air fryer takes the place of your microwave, oven, deep fryer, skillets, and more. Think about how much counter space that saves you—especially when you're lacking in space to begin with.

- Air fryers cook far faster than other cooking methods. Why? The air fryer's small cooking compartment is full of hot air. The hot air circulates around the food in the confined space, cooking the food rapidly. These machines are more energy-efficient than your full-sized oven too. Less space and a faster heating speed results in a lower utility bill.

- Air frying uses very little added fat. Rather than deep-frying in 2"–3" of oil, a quick spritz can produce beautiful fried foods with a satisfying crunch. Even if you're not dieting, this health benefit is a plus for any home cook.

- Cleanup is simple. Most air fryers have removable cooking baskets or trays. For simple meals, you can wipe out the tray or basket with a damp paper towel. For messier meals, you can wash the basket or tray in warm, soapy water or pop it in the dishwasher.

Choosing an Air Fryer

When choosing an air fryer, you'll find that models vary by size and style. The functionality is similar, but the differences can impact ease and frequency of use.

Size

Air fryers range in size from 1.2 quarts to 14 quarts. Because you are cooking for one, you may think the smallest size will work best. That may be true, especially if you have a small kitchen. However, if you have the space, a larger air fryer can make dinner prep a lot easier! If you're looking to make entire meals with an entrée and sides, you might want a 6-quart or larger fryer. Fryers this size will provide enough surface area for you to make multiple courses at once. For example, you can easily make a chicken breast with vegetables and a side of fries.

Style

There are two main styles of air fryer: basket and oven. They function the same way, and there is little to no difference in cooking time or level of difficulty for most foods. The basket style is more widely available and affordable. The oven style often has more surface area, which can allow you to cook more items in a single layer. An oven-style fryer often comes with a rotisserie and other attachments. Either style of air fryer will make your dinner prep fast and easy!

Air Fryer Functions

Most air fryers have buttons for types of cooking (e.g., bake, reheat, air fry) and/or types of food (e.g., chicken, pizza, wings). These buttons are programmed to preset times and temperatures based on your specific air fryer. Different brands may have different preset times. This book was created using manual times and temperatures instead of the presets.

Preheating

This is topic of frequent debate within the air fryer community. Some air fryers require preheating, and others do not. You should read the manual that comes with your air fryer and follow the instructions there. The recipes in this book were created *without* a preheating feature.

Helpful Accessories

The air fryer is an all-in-one tool, and you technically don't need to purchase accessories to make delicious food. That said, there are some useful tools that can make cooking with your air fryer more efficient. The following accessories will be used throughout this cookbook.

Olive Oil Sprayer

Some foods—especially breaded items—need a spritz of olive oil to brown properly. This is where a sprayer comes in. The preferred version is a refillable pump sprayer.

Aerosol Nonstick Spray

Most air fryers recommend that you do not use aerosol cooking sprays (e.g., PAM) because they can damage the nonstick finish. After many test runs, I have found that spraying just on the removable tray has not caused any damage to my air fryer. Do *not* spray the whole inside of the basket with the aerosol spray. You can spray any removable tray as long as you wash that tray after each use.

Silicone Tongs

Silicone tongs are one of the most useful accessories. They come in many thicknesses and lengths and can be long enough to turn any food. They will save you from burning yourself when reaching into the air fryer. Be sure to pick up one or more pairs that work best with your air fryer.

Ramekins

These small ceramic dishes are fantastic for making desserts or baked savory dishes for one. On Monday, you can make a lava cake in your ramekin, then on Tuesday you can make a savory egg dish using the same container. Throughout this cookbook, 4" ramekins that hold up to 8 ounces were used.

Pizza Pans

Deep-dish personal pizza pans (approximately 6"–7" diameter) can double as cake pans. They're also great if you're cooking something with a sauce and you don't want to lose said sauce through the grates of the air fryer.

Mini Loaf Pans

These are great for quick breads or meatloaf for one. Mini loaf pans are approximately 6" × 3" × 2" in size. You can find nonstick or silicone versions in-store or online. These pans are also great for mini casseroles.

Parchment Paper

A parchment paper lining makes for easy cleanup after using sticky ingredients. This material will be used in many recipes throughout the book. Depending on the size and shape of your air fryer, you can buy precut perforated sheets with holes for the air to pass through. Otherwise, you will have to cut the parchment paper to fit. Parchment paper will not burn unless heated to more than 500°F, which makes it air fryer safe.

Breading Trays

If you're craving a crispy fried treat but don't want the fat or calories, you can bread a vegetable and fry it in your air fryer. A set of three flat or low-sided breading trays makes food prep a lot easier. You can find these trays (plastic or metal) in many kitchen stores or online. Unlike a dinner plate, breading trays have sides to keep ingredients (like flour, egg, and panko) from making a mess. They also provide space to coat your food items more efficiently.

Spatulas

Spatulas of various sizes are helpful too. Depending on the size of your air fryer, you might sometimes need a skinny spatula to remove an item without disturbing adjacent food items. Other times, you may need a wider spatula to lift an item without breaking it.

Silicone Baking Cups

Baked goods such as cupcakes and biscuits handle better when you contain them in silicone cups. These baking cups are available in kitchen stores or online in a variety of colors to match your kitchen decor. Individual cups are also useful for making egg bites or fried eggs.

Instant-Read Meat Thermometer

How do you know if your meat is done? An instant-read meat thermometer reads the temperature of the meat right away. Just insert the thermometer into the thickest part of the protein to find out if your meat cooked properly. Instant-read thermometers are affordable (under $15) and easy to use.

Safety and Cleaning

Air fryers are safe and convenient when cooking for one, but they get very hot. Also, it's lucky that they're so easy to clean! Be sure you keep the following safe use practices in mind when using or cleaning your air fryer:

- Never get the housing or electrical components of your air fryer wet. Do not submerge electrical parts in water.
- You can clean the inside of the air fryer (where the heating element is) with a damp cloth when it's unplugged. Gently wipe the area down to remove any mess that you've made.
- Clean the inside of your air fryer by adding hot soapy water to the basket just above the tray level. Then, air fry at 350°F for 4 minutes. This process loosens any food residue, and you can use a sponge to remove the residue.
- Be sure your air fryer has 4"–5" of space around it on all sides, including on top and especially in back, so the air can properly vent during cooking.
- Unplug the air fryer when not in use.
- Be sure to use oven mitts when removing the basket or tray from the unit.

- Set the basket or tray on a trivet when you remove it from the unit. Otherwise, you could melt your countertop.
- Cook with the same temperature in half the time. Frozen foods can be frustrating because they rarely provide air fryer instructions. Use the temperature listed in the oven directions on the frozen package but reduce the cooking time by 50 percent. For example, if the oven directions for French fries are 425°F for 22 minutes, then you would air fry them at 425°F for 11 minutes.
- Don't overfill the air fryer. The hot air circulating around the food is the key to the food cooking evenly and quickly. If you overfill the basket or tray, you reduce the air circulation and the cooking temperature. Overcrowding causes your food to become less crisp.
- Pay attention to cooking times. If you are unsure how long to cook something, it is better to undercook the food. You can always add another minute or two of cooking time, but you can't unburn something! For example, if you want a medium-rare steak, cook the steak for the lowest number of minutes in the cooking time range. If the range is 9–13 minutes, cook it for 9 minutes. Then, check it with your meat thermometer. If it is too rare, add more cooking time. Also, browning can happen very quickly on foods like biscuits and French fries. You're better off choosing a shorter time frame, checking the items, and adding 1–2 minutes rather than overcooking and having to start over.

Clean the air fryer after each use to prevent lingering flavors or smells. You don't want your chocolate cake to smell like salmon!

Cooking for One Tips

Want to make the best use of your air fryer when you're cooking for one? Read the following advice to help you succeed.

- **Be on the lookout for individually packaged proteins.** There are a lot of options for chicken, fish, and other proteins that are vacuum sealed in individual packets. These preportioned servings are perfect when cooking for one. That said, if you buy a value pack, you can portion and freeze the extra servings in freezer-safe bags. By freezing them in individual servings, you can reduce food waste and save money.
- **Buy panko in bulk.** Panko bread crumbs are a popular ingredient because they add crunch without oil. They have a long shelf life, so you can buy a large economy bag to store for future use.
- **Get creative with bread.** Rather than using half a can of biscuits or half a piecrust, bread can be a very multipurpose ingredient. Bread slices can quickly become a hand piecrust or even an empanada wrapper.
- **Fresh fruit over canned.** Many times, recipes will call for canned fruit or pie filling. Rather than having half-cans of pie filling left over, use fresh fruit with a little sugar. The sugar will create a natural juice and the result is more nutritious and delicious!

- **Mini vegetables.** When cooking for one, you may only need ⅛ of a bell pepper. Buying mini vegetables, like bags of mini sweet peppers, is a great way to prevent food waste. Use green onions instead of a regular-sized onion, try mini cucumbers on a salad, and substitute Roma or grape tomatoes instead of a full-sized tomato. Most mushrooms are already the perfect size!
- **Pint-sized dairy products.** Nobody wants to throw away a half-gallon of milk because they didn't use it in time. Most grocery stores will have products like milk and buttermilk in pint containers.

With that, you're ready to start air frying! Throughout the following chapters, you'll find plenty of delicious recipes perfect when cooking for one. Let these recipes serve as your guide, but don't be afraid to customize dishes to your liking. Nutritional information will change as you alter recipes.

2

Breakfast

Breakfast is the most important meal of the day. No matter what's on the agenda, getting fuel in your body to start the day on the right foot is very important. Instead of hitting up a fast-food place on your way to work or activities, you can quickly make a delicious, filling breakfast at home in the air fryer, and you may even save time! No more waiting in line for 15 minutes, only to realize the line chef added tomatoes you didn't want on your breakfast sandwich.

This chapter has a wide variety of deliciously simple options for a breakfast for one. If you're looking for a picture worthy of social media, try the Avocado-Baked Eggs and pair it with some Candied Bacon. For the traditional breakfast lover, there's Fried Eggs that you can serve with Home Fries. If you love sweets, try the Peach Jam Breakfast Pie or the Blueberry Cheesecake Bread Pudding.

Avocado-Baked Eggs

The avocado peel serves as a nature-made bowl for a protein-rich egg in this fun breakfast. The creaminess of the avocado pairs deliciously with the mild egg flavor. Topping it with salsa is like making huevos rancheros without all the work! You can add some shredded cheese of your choice for extra flavor.

Hands-On Time: 5 minutes
Cook Time: 5 minutes

Serves 1

½ **large ripe avocado, pitted, peel intact**
1 **large egg**
1⁄16 **teaspoon salt**
1⁄16 **teaspoon ground black pepper**
1 **teaspoon salsa**
1 **teaspoon sour cream**

1   Scoop out some avocado flesh around the hole where the pit was to make it large enough to hold the cracked egg. Set this avocado flesh aside in a small bowl.

2   Place avocado half skin-side down in a ramekin. Crack egg into avocado half and sprinkle with salt and pepper.

3   Place ramekin in air fryer. Air fry at 350°F for 5–6 minutes for a runny egg or 6–7 minutes for a hard yolk.

4   Using tongs, carefully remove avocado half from air fryer. Top with salsa, sour cream, and reserved avocado. Serve.

PER SERVING

CALORIES: 194 | **FAT:** 15g | **SODIUM:** 261mg | **CARBOHYDRATES:** 7g | **FIBER:** 5g | **SUGAR:** 1g | **PROTEIN:** 8g

Hard-Boiled Eggs

Using an air fryer to hard-boil your eggs is quick and simple, and it doesn't even require water. You can then use these eggs for sandwiches, salads, and deviled eggs. For best results, peel the eggs right after the ice bath, rather than storing them in their shells.

Hands-On Time: 0 minutes
Cook Time: 15 minutes

Serves 1

2 large eggs

1 Carefully place eggs in air fryer. Air fry at 250°F for 15 minutes.

2 Transfer eggs to an ice bath and let cool 10 minutes. Peel and serve.

PER SERVING

CALORIES: 155 | **FAT:** 9g | **SODIUM:** 124mg | **CARBOHYDRATES:** 1g | **FIBER:** 0g | **SUGAR:** 1g | **PROTEIN:** 13g

French Toast

Light and fluffy air fryer French toast is a delicious and easy breakfast treat! You can even make a side of sausage or bacon at the same time. Swap out the heavy cream for half-and-half or milk for a subtle change. Top with butter and syrup or confectioners' sugar.

Hands-On Time: 5 minutes
Cook Time: 7 minutes

Serves 1

2 large eggs
2 tablespoons heavy cream
⅛ teaspoon coarse sea salt
¼ teaspoon ground cinnamon
¼ teaspoon vanilla extract
2 (¾"-thick) slices white bread

1 Open air fryer and cover air fryer tray with a fitted piece of parchment paper.

2 In a medium bowl, whisk together eggs, cream, salt, cinnamon, and vanilla.

3 Dip bread slices in egg mixture, making sure both sides are well coated. Lay bread slices in air fryer at least 1" apart. Air fry at 400°F for 4 minutes.

4 Open air fryer and flip bread slices. Air fry 3 minutes more. Remove French toast from air fryer and serve.

PER SERVING

CALORIES: 436 | **FAT:** 21g | **SODIUM:** 691mg | **CARBOHYDRATES:** 37g | **FIBER:** 2g | **SUGAR:** 5g | **PROTEIN:** 19g

Scotch Eggs

Air fryer Scotch eggs are a new favorite breakfast treat. If you're not familiar, a Scotch egg is sausage and eggs, all in one delightful crunchy bite! Dip it in ranch dressing, ketchup, or honey mustard dressing. For more information about how you can hard-boil eggs in the air fryer, see the previous recipe in this chapter.

Hands-On Time: 10 minutes
Cook Time: 14 minutes

Serves 1

⅓ pound bulk pork sausage
3 ounces full-fat cream cheese, softened
2 large hard-boiled eggs, peeled
¼ cup all-purpose flour
1 large egg, beaten
⅓ cup panko bread crumbs

HONEY MUSTARD DRESSING

Making honey mustard dressing just like your favorite restaurants serve is simple and tasty! Mix 1 tablespoon mayonnaise and 1 tablespoon honey mustard. You'll have that bright yellow, perfect honey mustard dressing that's great on salads or as a dip for these Scotch Eggs.

1 In a small bowl, mix sausage and cream cheese. Divide mixture into 2 portions and flatten each portion into a thin patty. Wrap each sausage patty around 1 hard-boiled egg, sealing all sides.

2 Prepare breading station with three medium dishes. Place flour in the first dish, beaten egg in the second dish, and panko in the third dish. Dip each sausage-wrapped egg into flour, then egg, and then panko, coating all sides.

3 Place sausage-wrapped eggs in air fryer. Spritz eggs with olive oil spray. Air fry at 400°F for 7 minutes.

4 Open air fryer, turn eggs, and spritz again with olive oil spray. Air fry 7 minutes more.

5 Carefully remove eggs from air fryer and serve.

PER SERVING

CALORIES: 831 | **FAT:** 43g | **SODIUM:** 611mg | **CARBOHYDRATES:** 37g | **FIBER:** 0g | **SUGAR:** 5g | **PROTEIN:** 57g

Fried Eggs

Frying an egg in an air fryer is so simple! It's versatile because you can cook the egg exactly how you like it, whether that's sunny-side up or well done. Nonstick cooking spray is essential to this recipe. A ramekin or any other small oven-safe dish works best.

Hands-On Time: 2 minutes
Cook Time: 5 minutes

Serves 1

1 large egg
1/16 teaspoon salt
1/16 teaspoon ground black pepper

1 Spray a ramekin with nonstick cooking spray.

2 Crack egg into ramekin and sprinkle with salt and pepper.

3 Place ramekin in air fryer. Air fry at 350°F for 5–6 minutes for a runny egg or 6–7 minutes for a hard yolk.

4 Using tongs and a pot holder, carefully remove ramekin from air fryer. Run a small silicone spatula around edges of ramekin and slip egg out.

PER SERVING

CALORIES: 77 | FAT: 4g | SODIUM: 207mg | CARBOHYDRATES: 1g | FIBER: 0g | SUGAR: 1g | PROTEIN: 6g

Candied Bacon

Candied bacon might be the only way to make bacon even better. Air frying bacon is very simple, and in this recipe, you'll top that bacon with a mixture of brown sugar and bacon grease. This topping adds an amazing sweetness and crunchy caramelization to your bacon. You could even try this Candied Bacon on a BLT.

Hands-On Time: 5 minutes
Cook Time: 16 minutes

Serves 1

3 strips bacon, cut in half
1½ tablespoons bacon grease
3 tablespoons light brown sugar

BACON GREASE ALTERNATIVES
If bacon grease isn't a mainstay in your kitchen, there are alternatives. You can purchase clarified bacon grease or use vegetable oil, shortening, or butter instead.

1 Lay out a sheet of parchment paper and scrunch up the sides all the way around to make a "basket" that will fit in your air fryer. The sides should be approximately 1"–2" high. Place parchment basket in air fryer. Poke holes in parchment for air to flow. This will help keep bacon from moving and will also keep your air fryer clean. Place bacon in parchment basket.

2 Place bacon grease in a small microwave-safe bowl and microwave for 45 seconds to melt. Add sugar and stir to form a paste.

3 Using a spoon, spread sugar mixture on bacon right away; otherwise, mixture will start to solidify.

4 Air fry at 325°F for 15 minutes.

5 Remove parchment basket from air fryer. Using a spatula, remove bacon from parchment and set on a medium plate. Let cool 5 minutes. Bacon will harden as it cools. Serve.

PER SERVING

CALORIES: 458 | FAT: 27g | SODIUM: 526mg | CARBOHYDRATES: 41g | FIBER: 0g | SUGAR: 40g | PROTEIN: 11g

Blueberry Cheesecake Bread Pudding

This Blueberry Cheesecake Bread Pudding could easily be featured as a dessert. Since it includes egg, bread, and fruit, it's also a wonderful choice for a decadent breakfast. The blueberries and sugar provide the perfect amount of sweetness to pair with the creaminess of the milk and cream cheese. It's delicious inside and out.

Hands-On Time: 5 minutes
Cook Time: 10 minutes

Serves 1

- 1 (¾"-thick) slice white bread, cut into ½" cubes, divided
- ¼ cup fresh blueberries, divided
- 1 ounce full-fat cream cheese, cut into ¼" cubes, divided
- 1 large egg
- ¼ cup 2% milk
- ½ teaspoon granulated sugar
- ½ teaspoon vanilla extract
- ¼ teaspoon ground cinnamon
- 1 teaspoon confectioners' sugar

CUSTOMIZE IT!

If you're not a fan of blueberries, you can use any fresh fruit that you like. Raspberries, peaches, or strawberries would work well with this bread pudding.

1 Spray a ramekin with nonstick cooking spray. Place half of bread cubes in ramekin.

2 Top with 2 tablespoons blueberries and half of cream cheese. Add remaining bread cubes, then remaining blueberries and remaining cream cheese.

3 In a small bowl, whisk together egg, milk, granulated sugar, vanilla, and cinnamon. Pour over bread cubes. Press down on blueberries, cream cheese, and bread so that bread soaks up egg mixture. Cover and refrigerate 10 minutes.

4 Place ramekin in air fryer. Air fry at 320°F for 10 minutes until bread cubes are golden brown.

5 Using pot holders, remove from air fryer, sprinkle with confectioners' sugar, and serve.

PER SERVING

CALORIES: 336 | FAT: 15g | SODIUM: 376mg | CARBOHYDRATES: 33g | FIBER: 2g | SUGAR: 12g | PROTEIN: 13g

Breakfast Crunch Wrap

Fast-food crunch wraps are fun and tasty but can be loaded with preservatives. Make your own wrap at home for a crunchy, cheesy breakfast. This breakfast does take time for prepping ingredients and cooking, but it's worth it! Feel free to use sausage instead of bacon or use your favorite cheese. Serve the wrap with more ranch and salsa.

Hands-On Time: 15 minutes
Cook Time: 14 minutes

Serves 1

- 1 large egg, beaten
- 2 strips bacon
- 1 (2-ounce) hash brown
- 1 (10") low-carb flour tortilla
- 2 tablespoons Mexican shredded cheese
- 2 tablespoons salsa
- 2 tablespoons ranch dressing
- 1 (6") low-carb flour tortilla

1 Spray a ramekin with nonstick cooking spray, then pour beaten egg into ramekin. Open air fryer and place bacon, hash brown, and ramekin inside. Air fry at 350°F for 5–7 minutes until egg no longer runs.

2 Open air fryer and remove ramekin using tongs or a pot holder. Close and air fry bacon and hash brown 4 minutes more.

3 Lay large tortilla on a cutting board. Using a small silicone spatula, spoon scrambled egg onto center of tortilla. Top with cheese, salsa, and ranch dressing.

4 When cook time is up, open air fryer. Remove hash brown and bacon with tongs and place on top of salsa and ranch dressing. Lay small tortilla on top of stack. Fold up excess sides of large tortilla on top of small tortilla to make a hexagon shape. Spritz lightly with olive oil spray while holding the fold.

5 Place wrap folded-side down in air fryer. Spritz top of wrap with olive oil spray. Air fry at 350°F for 5 minutes.

6 Remove from air fryer and serve.

PER SERVING

CALORIES: 507 | **FAT:** 31g | **SODIUM:** 1,484mg | **CARBOHYDRATES:** 44g | **FIBER:** 22g | **SUGAR:** 4g | **PROTEIN:** 28g

Cinnamon French Toast Rolls

Return to childhood with this fun finger-food breakfast. These French toast rolls are crunchy, sweet, and delicious! The rolls need just a few ingredients and are ready in minutes. Dip these rolls in syrup for a touch of added sweetness!

Hands-On Time: 5 minutes
Cook Time: 6 minutes

Serves 1

- 2 (¾"-thick) slices white bread
- 1 tablespoon salted butter, softened
- 1 teaspoon ground cinnamon
- 1 teaspoon granulated sugar
- 1 large egg
- 2 teaspoons 2% milk
- 1 tablespoon confectioners' sugar

CONFECTIONERS' SUGAR SHAKER

You can find shaker or sifter gadgets for confectioners' sugar at most kitchen stores. You can also use a hand sifter to lightly shake confectioners' sugar on top of these yummy roll-ups!

1 Lay bread slices on a cutting board. With a rolling pin, flatten bread slices.

2 Spread butter on top of bread slices. Sprinkle cinnamon and granulated sugar on bread. Tightly roll up each slice.

3 In a small bowl, beat together egg and milk. Roll bread rolls in egg mixture.

4 Open air fryer and lightly spray air fryer basket with nonstick cooking spray. Place rolls in air fryer and air fry at 350°F for 6 minutes.

5 Using tongs, carefully remove rolls from air fryer. Sprinkle with confectioners' sugar and serve.

PER SERVING

CALORIES: 416 | **FAT:** 17g | **SODIUM:** 510mg | **CARBOHYDRATES:** 50g | **FIBER:** 3g | **SUGAR:** 16g | **PROTEIN:** 13g

English Muffin Breakfast Pizza

Who hasn't had a hankering for a slice of pizza in the morning? The best thing about any pizza, this one included, is that you can customize it however you like: Swap bacon for sausage, add vegetables, and more. English muffins provide the perfect single-serving pizza crust and get crunchy quickly in the air fryer. Use bagels instead for a thicker base.

Hands-On Time: 2 minutes
Cook Time: 10 minutes

Serves 1

1 large egg
1 tablespoon 2% milk
⅛ teaspoon salt
⅛ teaspoon ground black pepper
2 (1½-ounce) frozen fully cooked sausage patties
1 English muffin, split in half
¼ cup shredded Colby jack cheese
⅛ teaspoon garlic salt

1 In a small bowl, whisk together egg, milk, salt, and pepper.

2 Spray a ramekin with nonstick cooking spray. Pour egg mixture into ramekin.

3 Open air fryer and place ramekin and sausage patties inside. Air fry at 350°F for 5 minutes.

4 Open air fryer and, using tongs, remove sausage patties. Close air fryer and air fry egg 2 minutes more.

5 Using pot holders, remove ramekin from air fryer. Chop cooked scrambled egg and sausage patties into bite-sized pieces.

6 Place English muffin halves in air fryer. Spritz muffin lightly with olive oil spray.

7 Top muffin with scrambled egg, sausage, Colby jack, and garlic salt. Air fry at 350°F for 3 minutes to melt cheese.

8 Using a spatula, carefully remove pizzas from air fryer and serve.

PER SERVING

CALORIES: 449 | **FAT:** 26g | **SODIUM:** 1,054mg | **CARBOHYDRATES:** 27g | **FIBER:** 2g | **SUGAR:** 3g | **PROTEIN:** 23g

Cheesy Mushroom Egg Bites

Egg bites are a versatile breakfast. Making them is also a great way to use up small amounts of leftovers you might have in your refrigerator. You can easily replace the mushrooms with any leftover meats or vegetables. You can double the recipe and have extras for breakfast tomorrow.

Hands-On Time: 5 minutes
Cook Time: 13 minutes

Serves 1

4 mushrooms, diced
1 large egg
1 large egg white
2 tablespoons cottage cheese
2 tablespoons shredded Colby jack cheese
½ teaspoon hot sauce
1⁄16 teaspoon salt
1⁄16 teaspoon ground black pepper

CUSTOMIZE IT

If you're not a mushroom fan, you can easily customize these egg bites with any other chopped vegetables, such as bell peppers or diced onions. You could also add diced ham or crumbled bacon.

1 Place mushrooms in a ramekin. Spritz with olive oil spray, then place ramekin in air fryer. Air fry mushrooms at 350°F for 3 minutes.

2 In a medium bowl, using an electric hand mixer on low speed, mix all other ingredients.

3 Spray three silicone baking cups with non-stick cooking spray. You can also use a small muffin tin or small ramekins, depending on the size and shape of your air fryer basket. Pour egg mixture into baking cups. Using pot holders, remove ramekin with mushrooms from air fryer and sprinkle into baking cups.

4 Pour ½ cup water into bottom of air fryer, below basket. This helps the eggs steam as they cook.

5 Place baking cups on air fryer tray. Air fry at 300°F for 10 minutes.

6 Using tongs, carefully remove cups from air fryer. Run a butter knife around edges of egg bites to remove from baking cups and serve.

PER SERVING

CALORIES: 231 | **FAT:** 10g | **SODIUM:** 547mg | **CARBOHYDRATES:** 11g | **FIBER:** 3g | **SUGAR:** 7g | **PROTEIN:** 25g

Peach Jam Breakfast Pie

This breakfast pie is a fun way to make a quick and fruit-filled start to your day. This is not an oven-baked crusted pie; instead, it's composed of bread, peach, and a few other ingredients. Recipes for this type of pie usually make a big batch, but with a few tricks you can make one serving! It's an homage to summertime that you can enjoy year-round.

Hands-On Time: 5 minutes
Cook Time: 7 minutes

Serves 1

- 2 (¾"-thick) slices white bread
- 2 tablespoons salted butter, softened
- 2 teaspoons peach jam
- 1 teaspoon ground cinnamon
- 1 teaspoon light brown sugar
- 1 small peach, peeled and thinly sliced
- 1 large egg, beaten
- 3 tablespoons confectioners' sugar
- ½ teaspoon 2% milk

1. Lay bread slices on a cutting board. With a rolling pin, flatten bread slices. Spread butter and jam on top of bread slices, then sprinkle cinnamon and brown sugar on top.

2. Place half of peach slices on bottom half of each bread slice. Fold bread slice over peaches and, using a fork, seal the edges. Using a pastry brush, lightly brush beaten egg onto sealed hand pies.

3. Open air fryer and lightly spray tray with nonstick cooking spray. Place pies in air fryer and air fry at 350°F for 7 minutes.

4. While pies are cooking, in a small bowl, mix confectioners' sugar and milk to make a quick icing.

5. Using a spatula, carefully remove pies from air fryer. Drizzle pies with icing and serve.

PER SERVING

CALORIES: 659 | **FAT:** 28g | **SODIUM:** 603mg | **CARBOHYDRATES:** 87g | **FIBER:** 5g | **SUGAR:** 49g | **PROTEIN:** 14g

Breakfast Burrito

Breakfast Burritos are fantastic because you can take them on the go to work or when heading out for fun! They also freeze well. If freezing, wrap in aluminum foil and then place in a freezer bag. Remove from freezer and air fry (with foil on) at 350°F for 5 minutes. Serve with salsa and sour cream.

Hands-On Time: 5 minutes
Cook Time: 10 minutes

Serves 1

1 large egg
2 tablespoons 2% milk
⅟₁₆ teaspoon salt
⅟₁₆ teaspoon ground black pepper
1 (1½-ounce) frozen fully cooked sausage patty
1 (6") low-carb flour tortilla
2 tablespoons shredded pepper jack cheese
2 tablespoons salsa

1 In a small bowl, whisk together egg, milk, salt, and pepper.

2 Spray a ramekin with nonstick cooking spray. Pour egg mixture into ramekin. Open air fryer and place ramekin and sausage patty in air fryer basket. Air fry at 350°F for 4 minutes.

3 Open air fryer, stir eggs, and flip patty. Air fry 3 minutes more. Open air fryer and, using tongs, remove ramekin and sausage patty.

4 Lay out tortilla and spoon scrambled eggs onto tortilla. Break up sausage patty and add on top of egg. Top with pepper jack and salsa.

5 Fold sides of tortilla into center, then fold up bottom of tortilla and roll into a burrito. Place burrito in air fryer and spritz with olive oil spray. Air fry at 350°F for 3 minutes to melt cheese and crisp tortilla.

6 Using tongs, carefully remove burrito from air fryer and serve.

PER SERVING

CALORIES: 347 | FAT: 23g | SODIUM: 1,092mg | CARBOHYDRATES: 19g | FIBER: 10g | SUGAR: 3g | PROTEIN: 20g

Home Fries

These delicious Home Fries only call for a potato and a couple of basic seasonings. Home Fries pair well with fried or scrambled eggs. Add cheese for the last 2 minutes of cook time for an even tastier breakfast side.

Hands-On Time: 5 minutes
Cook Time: 12 minutes

Serves 1

1 small russet potato, cut into ½" cubes
1 tablespoon olive oil
1/16 teaspoon salt
1/16 teaspoon ground black pepper
1/16 teaspoon garlic salt

1 In a medium bowl, toss together potato, oil, salt, pepper, and garlic salt.

2 Pour potatoes into a single layer in air fryer. Air fry at 400°F for 7 minutes.

3 Open air fryer and shake basket to toss home fries. Air fry 5 minutes more. Using a spatula, remove home fries from air fryer and serve.

PER SERVING

CALORIES: 252 | **FAT:** 13g | **SODIUM:** 286mg | **CARBOHYDRATES:** 30g | **FIBER:** 3g | **SUGAR:** 1g | **PROTEIN:** 4g

Ham and Cheese Omelet

An omelet is an easy breakfast when you have an air fryer! You can change up your omelet by adding sausage, peppers, onions, and spinach. Serve with toast and jam.

Hands-On Time: 3 minutes
Cook Time: 9 minutes

Serves 1

2 large eggs
2 tablespoons 2% milk
⅛ teaspoon hot sauce
1/16 teaspoon salt
1/16 teaspoon ground black pepper
3 slices shaved deli ham
2 tablespoons shredded Colby jack cheese

1 In a medium bowl, whisk together eggs, milk, hot sauce, salt, and pepper.

2 Spray a 6" cake pan with nonstick cooking spray. Pour egg mixture into pan. Sprinkle ham and Colby jack into egg mixture. Place pan in air fryer, removing tray and placing pan in bottom of air fryer basket if needed.

3 Air fry at 320°F for 9 minutes. Using tongs, carefully remove cake pan from air fryer. Slip omelet out of pan and serve.

PER SERVING

CALORIES: 252 | **FAT:** 15g | **SODIUM:** 746mg | **CARBOHYDRATES:** 3g | **FIBER:** 0g | **SUGAR:** 1g | **PROTEIN:** 23g

Nutty Buddy Granola

Granola is a great grab-and-go breakfast or snack during the day. Make this batch in minutes. Double it and you'll have enough for a couple of days! Customize it by adding other dried fruit if you'd like, or serve it with fresh fruit and milk for a homemade cereal.

Hands-On Time: 5 minutes
Cook Time: 7 minutes

Serves 1

- ⅓ cup old-fashioned rolled oats
- 1 tablespoon chopped pecans
- ½ tablespoon maple syrup
- ½ tablespoon salted butter, softened
- ¼ teaspoon vanilla extract
- ¹⁄₁₆ teaspoon salt
- 1 tablespoon peanut butter chips
- 1 tablespoon dried cranberries, chopped

1 In a medium bowl, toss oats, pecans, syrup, butter, vanilla, and salt.

2 Line air fryer basket with parchment paper and poke a few holes in parchment for air to pass through. Pour oat mixture into a single layer on parchment. Air fry at 325°F for 4 minutes.

3 Open air fryer and shake basket to lightly toss granola. Lower temperature to 300°F and air fry 3 minutes more.

4 Pour granola into a medium bowl. Let cool completely, 20–30 minutes.

5 Fold in peanut butter chips and cranberries and serve.

PER SERVING

CALORIES: 311 | **FAT:** 17g | **SODIUM:** 220mg | **CARBOHYDRATES:** 36g | **FIBER:** 4g | **SUGAR:** 14g | **PROTEIN:** 7g

Bull's-Eye Egg

Crack an egg in the middle of a piece of toast, and voilà—a recipe that has stood the test of time. It's delicious, and you can easily make it in your air fryer. With just a couple of ingredients, this breakfast is perfect when you're hungry but short on time.

Hands-On Time: 2 minutes
Cook Time: 8 minutes

Serves 1

1 teaspoon salted butter
1 (¾"-thick) slice white bread
1 large egg
¹⁄₁₆ teaspoon salt
¹⁄₁₆ teaspoon ground black pepper

1 Lay a sheet of parchment paper in the bottom of your air fryer basket.

2 Spread butter on top of bread. Using the bottom of a drinking glass, press a circle indentation into center of bread but do not cut through bread. Place bread slice buttered-side up in air fryer.

3 Crack egg into indentation in bread. Sprinkle with salt and pepper. Air fry at 320°F for 5 minutes.

4 Carefully flip toast with egg (yolk may break). Air fry 3 minutes more.

5 Using a spatula, carefully remove toast and egg from air fryer and serve.

PER SERVING

CALORIES: 197 | **FAT:** 9g | **SODIUM:** 417mg | **CARBOHYDRATES:** 18g | **FIBER:** 1g | **SUGAR:** 2g | **PROTEIN:** 9g

Loaded Breakfast Casserole

Some days a quick granola bar from the cupboard just isn't enough. This hearty breakfast casserole is loaded with all your favorite breakfast ingredients! A small casserole dish, approximately 4" × 4", or a mini loaf pan is best for this breakfast for one.

Hands-On Time: 5 minutes
Cook Time: 14 minutes

Serves 1

2 strips bacon
1 (1½-ounce) frozen fully cooked sausage patty
1 (2-ounce) frozen hash brown
2 large eggs
3 tablespoons half-and-half
2 tablespoons shredded Cheddar cheese
1 mini sweet pepper, diced
1 tablespoon diced white onion
⅛ teaspoon hot sauce
1/16 teaspoon salt
1/16 teaspoon ground black pepper

1 Place bacon, sausage patty, and hash brown in air fryer. Air fry at 350°F for 4 minutes. This will parcook each of these ingredients. Spray a small baking dish with nonstick cooking spray.

2 In a medium bowl, whisk together eggs, half-and-half, Cheddar, mini sweet pepper, onion, hot sauce, salt, and black pepper.

3 Open air fryer and remove bacon, sausage, and hash brown. Chop bacon and sausage into bite-sized pieces.

4 Lay hash brown on bottom of prepared dish. Sprinkle bacon and sausage pieces into dish, then pour egg mixture into dish. Place dish in air fryer, removing tray and placing dish in bottom of basket if needed. Air fry at 300°F for 5 minutes.

5 Open air fryer. Using a spatula, pull sides of casserole in and lift slightly; uncooked portions of egg will run out into dish. Air fry 5 minutes more.

6 Using tongs, carefully remove dish from air fryer. Let cool 2–3 minutes before serving.

PER SERVING

CALORIES: 533 | **FAT:** 35g | **SODIUM:** 1,047mg | **CARBOHYDRATES:** 16g | **FIBER:** 1g | **SUGAR:** 4g | **PROTEIN:** 31g

Bacon, Egg, and Cheese Biscuit Bombs

Individually frozen biscuits are a great way to make these biscuit bombs in a small quantity. Thaw out a couple of biscuits in your refrigerator. Then fill them with your favorite toppings!

Hands-On Time: 5 minutes
Cook Time: 21 minutes

Serves 1

2 strips bacon, cut in half
1 large egg
2 tablespoons 2% milk
1⁄16 teaspoon salt
1⁄16 teaspoon ground black pepper
2 frozen buttermilk biscuits, thawed 1–2 days
2 tablespoons shredded Colby jack cheese

1 Place bacon in air fryer and air fry at 350°F for 3 minutes.

2 Spray a ramekin with nonstick cooking spray. In a small bowl, whisk together egg, milk, salt, and pepper. Pour egg mixture into ramekin.

3 Open air fryer and place ramekin inside. Air fry at 350°F for 4 minutes. Open air fryer and remove bacon. Break up egg with a fork, then air fry 3 minutes more.

4 While eggs are cooking, using a rolling pin, roll each biscuit into a thin 4" round.

5 Open air fryer and, with a pot holder, remove ramekin. Break up egg with fork into bite-sized pieces. Spoon half of scrambled egg onto center of each flattened biscuit. Top each biscuit with half of bacon and Colby jack. Pull sides of biscuit up around toppings and pinch to seal. Gently roll biscuit in your hand so it's completely sealed and round.

6 Line air fryer basket with parchment paper. Put biscuit bombs on parchment and spritz outside of biscuit bombs with olive oil spray. Air fry at 325°F for 8 minutes.

7 Open air fryer and flip biscuit bombs. Spritz other side with olive oil spray. Air fry 3 minutes more. Using tongs, carefully remove bombs from air fryer and serve.

PER SERVING

CALORIES: 463 | **FAT:** 22g | **SODIUM:** 1,299mg | **CARBOHYDRATES:** 40g | **FIBER:** 1g | **SUGAR:** 3g | **PROTEIN:** 22g

Strawberry Scones

These fruity scones are a comforting twist on regular biscuits. Top with icing or serve with butter for a delightful breakfast today and tomorrow—if you can resist eating them all at once! Substitute blueberries for the strawberries if you prefer.

Hands-On Time: 10 minutes
Cook Time: 8 minutes

Serves 2

Scones
4 strawberries, diced
3 teaspoons granulated sugar, divided
½ cup plus 2 tablespoon all-purpose flour, plus extra for sprinkling
½ teaspoon baking powder
⅛ teaspoon salt
⅛ teaspoon baking soda
2 tablespoons cold salted butter, diced
2 tablespoons 2% milk
1 large egg yolk

Glaze
6 tablespoons confectioners' sugar
1 teaspoon 2% milk

1 To make Scones: In a small bowl, toss strawberries with ¼ teaspoon sugar. Set aside.

2 In a medium bowl, stir together flour, baking powder, salt, baking soda, and remaining 2¾ teaspoons sugar. Using a fork, mix butter into flour mixture until mixture is crumbly.

3 In a small bowl, whisk together milk and egg yolk. Fold egg mixture into flour mixture and stir until combined. Fold in strawberries and any accumulated juice.

4 Sprinkle cutting board generously with extra flour. Remove dough from bowl and place on floured cutting board. Knead dough lightly into a 4" circle about 1" thick. Add more flour if dough is sticky. Using a round cookie cutter, cut 3 Scones out of dough. After each round is cut, you may need to reform dough into a circle.

5 Line air fryer basket with parchment paper. Place dough rounds on parchment. Air fry at 400°F for 8 minutes.

6 To make Glaze: In a small bowl, whisk together sugar and milk until smooth.

7 Using tongs, carefully transfer Scones to a wire rack. Let cool 5 minutes. Spoon Glaze over Scones once cooled.

PER SERVING

CALORIES: 403 | **FAT:** 14g | **SODIUM:** 449mg | **CARBOHYDRATES:** 63g | **FIBER:** 2g | **SUGAR:** 31g | **PROTEIN:** 6g

Applesauce Coffee Cake

Coffee cake is delicious when served warm with a cup of coffee any day of the week. The applesauce adds a nice sweetness and goes great with the cinnamon flavor of the cake. Plus, this cake is the perfect size for one!

Hands-On Time: 10 minutes
Cook Time: 20 minutes

Serves 1

Cake
⅓ cup all-purpose flour
2 tablespoons granulated sugar
1 tablespoon light brown sugar
½ teaspoon baking powder
¼ teaspoon salt
¼ teaspoon ground cinnamon
⅛ teaspoon ground nutmeg
4 teaspoons applesauce
2 tablespoons salted butter, melted
1 large egg yolk
3 tablespoons 2% milk

Streusel
1 tablespoon salted butter, softened
2 tablespoons light brown sugar
½ teaspoon granulated sugar
¼ teaspoon ground cinnamon
2 tablespoons all-purpose flour

1 Spray a 4" × 4" baking dish with nonstick cooking spray.

2 To make Cake: In a medium bowl, whisk together flour, both sugars, baking powder, salt, cinnamon, and nutmeg. In a separate medium bowl, whisk together applesauce, butter, egg yolk, and milk.

3 Add applesauce mixture to flour mixture and stir until combined. Pour batter into prepared dish.

4 To make Streusel: In a small bowl, combine butter, both sugars, cinnamon, and flour. Mix with a fork until a crumbly mixture forms. Sprinkle over top of batter in dish and press lightly so mixture sticks. Cover dish tightly with aluminum foil.

5 Place dish in air fryer. Air fry at 300°F for 10 minutes. Open air fryer and remove foil. Air fry 10 minutes more.

6 Open air fryer and check Cake for doneness with a toothpick. Toothpick inserted in center of Cake should come out clean. If needed, air fry 3–5 minutes more.

7 Using a pot holder, carefully remove dish from air fryer. Let cool 5 minutes before serving.

PER SERVING

CALORIES: 860 | **FAT:** 38g | **SODIUM:** 1,138mg | **CARBOHYDRATES:** 118g | **FIBER:** 3g | **SUGAR:** 69g | **PROTEIN:** 11g

Silver Dollar Pancakes

Silver dollar pancakes are quick and easy to make. These golden-brown mini pancakes are light, fluffy, and buttery. Top them off with butter and syrup and they're a perfect breakfast.

Hands-On Time: 10 minutes
Cook Time: 7 minutes

Serves 1

- ½ cup all-purpose flour
- ½ teaspoon baking powder
- 1 teaspoon granulated sugar
- ⅛ teaspoon sea salt
- ½ large egg
- ½ cup 2% milk
- 2 teaspoons salted butter, melted

1 In a large mixing bowl, combine flour, baking powder, sugar, and salt. Whisk to combine.

2 In a medium bowl, beat egg and milk, then add butter. Pour egg mixture into flour mixture and gently stir until just combined.

3 Set batter aside. Place four ramekins in air fryer and heat at 360°F for 5 minutes. Open air fryer and spray ramekins with nonstick cooking spray. Using a cookie scoop, divide batter among ramekins, spreading batter to edges of ramekins.

4 Air fry for 7–8 minutes until pancakes are golden brown. Using a rubber spatula, slip pancakes out of ramekins and serve.

PER SERVING

CALORIES: 408 | **FAT:** 12g | **SODIUM:** 499mg | **CARBOHYDRATES:** 59g | **FIBER:** 2g | **SUGAR:** 4g | **PROTEIN:** 14g

3

Appetizers and Snacks

When cooking for one, it's important to remember that you are worth the effort! Using your air fryer to make delicious appetizers and snacks may seem like a hassle, but they are actually easy and fast to make. Some of these appetizers could even be a full meal on a day when you're not too hungry. Either way, these dishes will hit the spot. There are even a few take-away snack ideas for when you are running late for the office, heading out the door to watch a niece's baseball game, or throwing yourself a picnic in the park.

This chapter reads like the appetizer menu at your favorite bar. You have classic options like Potato Skins, a creamy Stuffed Portobello Mushroom, and spicy Bacon-Wrapped Taco-Stuffed Jalapeño Poppers. Try something new with mouthwatering Buffalo Cauliflower Wings or Spicy Ranch Chickpeas. You won't know what to devour first!

Pimento Cheese Sausage Balls

Looking for a cheesy and meat-filled appetizer? These Pimento Cheese Sausage Balls will make you wish you had made a double portion! Adding pimento cheese makes these sausage balls even more flavor-packed. Serve with ranch or honey mustard. You may use Bisquick as your baking mix.

Hands-On Time: 10 minutes
Cook Time: 10 minutes

Serves 1

2 ounces full-fat cream cheese, softened
1 tablespoon mayonnaise
½ teaspoon garlic salt
¼ cup shredded sharp Cheddar cheese
1 tablespoon diced pimento
¼ pound bulk pork sausage, broken up into small pieces
⅓ cup baking mix

1 In a medium bowl, use a spatula to mix cream cheese, mayonnaise, garlic salt, Cheddar, and pimento. Add sausage and stir to combine. Add baking mix and mix well.

2 Line a small baking sheet with parchment paper. Using a medium cookie scoop, scoop balls of sausage mixture and place on parchment. Freeze balls for 15 minutes.

3 Remove sheet from freezer and roll balls to make them rounder.

4 Line air fryer tray with parchment and spray with nonstick cooking spray. Poke holes in parchment for oil to drain. Place balls in air fryer and air fry at 370°F for 5 minutes. Open air fryer and turn balls with silicone tongs. Air fry 5 minutes more.

5 Using tongs, carefully remove balls from air fryer and serve.

PER SERVING

CALORIES: 758 | **FAT:** 67g | **SODIUM:** 2,583mg | **CARBOHYDRATES:** 30g | **FIBER:** 0g | **SUGAR:** 9g | **PROTEIN:** 26g

Stuffed Portobello Mushroom

Stuffed portobello mushrooms are a very popular appetizer at Italian restaurants. They are surprisingly easy to make, and you can stuff them with all sorts of cheeses. This is great as an appetizer or even as a vegetarian main dish.

Hands-On Time: 10 minutes
Cook Time: 8 minutes

Serves 1

2 tablespoons ricotta cheese
2 tablespoons shredded mozzarella cheese
1 tablespoon bread crumbs
⅛ teaspoon Italian seasoning
¹⁄₁₆ teaspoon garlic salt
1 large portobello mushroom, stemmed
1 tablespoon salted butter, melted

1 In a medium bowl, stir ricotta, mozzarella, bread crumbs, Italian seasoning, and garlic salt until well combined.

2 Place cheese mixture inside mushroom cavity so that mushroom is slightly overstuffed. Place stuffed mushroom in air fryer and pour butter over mushroom. Air fry at 350°F for 8 minutes.

3 Remove mushroom from air fryer and let cool 1–2 minutes. Serve.

PER SERVING

CALORIES: 230 | **FAT:** 17g | **SODIUM:** 368mg | **CARBOHYDRATES:** 10g | **FIBER:** 2g | **SUGAR:** 3g | **PROTEIN:** 9g

Potato Skins

These mouthwatering Potato Skins are just like the ones at your favorite sports bar, topped with cheese, bacon, and sour cream. Parcooking the potatoes helps speed up the cooking time.

Hands-On Time: 15 minutes
Cook Time: 27 minutes

Serves 1

3 strips bacon, cut in half
3 small red potatoes
1 tablespoon olive oil, divided
1 teaspoon coarse sea salt, divided
½ cup shredded Colby jack cheese
2 tablespoons sour cream
1 green onion, sliced
2 teaspoons seasoning salt

PRECOOKED BACON

If you'd like to save a little time in this recipe, you can use precooked bacon. You can dice it and add it on top of the cheese before you air fry.

1 Place bacon in air fryer. Air fry at 400°F for 10 minutes.

2 While bacon is cooking, cut slits in potatoes with a paring knife. Wrap potatoes in a wet paper towel and microwave for 5 minutes. Potatoes are done when a knife slides in easily. Place in refrigerator to cool.

3 Remove bacon from air fryer and place on a paper towel.

4 Slice cooled potatoes in half lengthwise. Using a metal spoon, carefully scoop out about half of potato flesh. Set this potato flesh aside for use in another recipe. Leave a ¼" ridge of flesh around each potato half.

5 Place potatoes cut-side down in air fryer. Sprinkle with ½ tablespoon oil and ½ teaspoon sea salt. Air fry at 375°F for 5 minutes.

6 Open air fryer, flip potatoes cut-side up, and sprinkle with remaining ½ tablespoon oil and remaining ½ teaspoon sea salt. Air fry 4 minutes more.

7 While potatoes are cooking, chop bacon.

8 When potatoes are done, open air fryer and add Colby jack, pushing it into potatoes so it doesn't blow around while cooking. Air fry at 375°F for 3 minutes until cheese has melted.

9 Using tongs, remove potato skins from air fryer. Top with bacon, sour cream, green onion, and seasoning salt. Serve.

PER SERVING

CALORIES: 639 | FAT: 44g | SODIUM: 5,470mg | CARBOHYDRATES: 30g | FIBER: 3g | SUGAR: 4g | PROTEIN: 28g

Spicy Ranch Chickpeas

Crunchy chickpeas are a fun and tasty snack—plus, they're healthy! If you're not a fan of spicy food, you can customize these with whatever spices you like. These crunchy chickpeas are like a bowl of popcorn! Aquafaba is the drained liquid from a can of chickpeas—so make sure not to drain the chickpea juice and throw it away!

Hands-On Time: 5 minutes
Cook Time: 12 minutes

Serves 1

½ (15-ounce) can chickpeas
1 tablespoon aquafaba
½ teaspoon ranch seasoning mix
½ teaspoon chili powder
¼ teaspoon coarse sea salt

1 Drain chickpeas over a small bowl, careful to not pour out all aquafaba. Do not rinse chickpeas.

2 Place chickpeas in air fryer basket in a single layer. Air fry at 400°F for 7 minutes.

3 In a medium bowl, whisk together aquafaba, ranch seasoning, and chili powder.

4 Open air fryer and pour chickpeas into the bowl with seasoning mixture. Toss to coat evenly.

5 Scoop seasoned chickpeas back into air fryer tray in a single layer. Air fry 5 minutes more, checking every 2 minutes to be sure they don't burn. Take them out when they reach your desired crunchy consistency.

6 Pour chickpeas into serving dish and sprinkle with salt. Serve.

PER SERVING

CALORIES: 183 | **FAT:** 2g | **SODIUM:** 967mg | **CARBOHYDRATES:** 33g | **FIBER:** 9g | **SUGAR:** 6g | **PROTEIN:** 10g

Pizza Snack Rolls with Garlic Parmesan Butter

After you make these Pizza Snack Rolls once, you'll be craving them every day! Cooking premade frozen foods in an air fryer can be confusing because the packaging lacks specific instructions for this appliance. This recipe will help you prepare pizza snack rolls and take them to the next level by tossing them in garlic Parmesan butter.

Hands-On Time: 2 minutes
Cook Time: 7 minutes

Serves 1

- 10 frozen pizza snack rolls
- 2 tablespoons salted butter, softened
- ¼ teaspoon minced garlic
- 2 teaspoons grated Parmesan cheese

1 Place snack rolls in air fryer. Air fry at 400°F for 4 minutes.

2 Open air fryer and flip snack rolls, then air fry 2 minutes more.

3 While snack rolls are cooking, place butter and garlic in a small microwave-safe bowl. Microwave 20 seconds until melted.

4 Remove snack rolls from air fryer and place them in a medium bowl. Pour garlic butter over rolls and toss.

5 Top with Parmesan and serve.

PER SERVING

CALORIES: 657 | **FAT:** 34g | **SODIUM:** 1,053mg | **CARBOHYDRATES:** 68g | **FIBER:** 2g | **SUGAR:** 5g | **PROTEIN:** 13g

Stuffed Mini Peppers

These air fryer Stuffed Mini Peppers are a tasty treat that are great as an appetizer or a meal. Filled with sausage, cream cheese, and more, they're a savory sensation. They are done so quickly that you may run back to the air fryer for round two. Serve with ranch dressing.

Hands-On Time: 8 minutes
Cook Time: 8 minutes

Serves 1

- 2 tablespoons full-fat cream cheese
- 1 ounce bulk Italian sausage
- ⅛ teaspoon garlic powder
- 2 tablespoons shredded Colby jack cheese
- ⅛ teaspoon Worcestershire sauce
- 2 mini sweet peppers, trimmed and halved lengthwise, seeds and membranes removed

1   In a medium bowl, using a wooden spoon, mash together cream cheese, sausage, garlic powder, Colby jack, and Worcestershire sauce.

2   Fill peppers with sausage mixture using a spoon. The amount will vary based on the pepper size. You may overstuff peppers if you have extra filling.

3   Place peppers in air fryer basket and air fry at 360°F for 8 minutes until cheese is melted and bubbly.

4   Remove from air fryer and let cool slightly before serving.

PER SERVING

CALORIES: 249 | **FAT:** 20g | **SODIUM:** 373mg | **CARBOHYDRATES:** 5g | **FIBER:** 1g | **SUGAR:** 3g | **PROTEIN:** 9g

Tostones and Guacamole

People in many South American countries have plantains with every meal. One very popular way to eat them is to make them into tostones, or fried chips. Plantains are similar to bananas, but they are starchier and not quite as sweet, which is why tostones are delicious. This recipe pairs these chips with a simple, quick guacamole.

Hands-On Time: 2 minutes
Cook Time: 12 minutes

Serves 1

Tostones
½ tablespoon olive oil
½ tablespoon sazón
    seasoning mix
1 small plantain, peeled and
    sliced ¼" thick

Guacamole
½ medium ripe avocado,
    pitted, peel intact
4 tablespoons pico de gallo
½ teaspoon salt
Juice of 1 medium lime

1 To make Tostones: Place oil and sazón in a medium bowl. Add plantains and toss until they are coated on all sides.

2 Lay plantain slices in air fryer basket in a single layer. Air fry at 350°F for 6 minutes.

3 To make Guacamole: Scoop out avocado into a small bowl and mash. Add pico de gallo, salt, and lime juice and mash together. Cover and refrigerate until ready to serve with Tostones.

4 Remove plantains from air fryer and place on a cutting board. Using the bottom of a drinking glass, smash plantain chips so they are thinner. Return chips to air fryer and air fry 6 minutes more.

5 Remove from air fryer and serve warm with Guacamole.

PER SERVING

CALORIES: 412 | **FAT:** 16g | **SODIUM:** 2,494mg | **CARBOHYDRATES:** 70g | **FIBER:** 9g | **SUGAR:** 31g | **PROTEIN:** 4g

Buffalo Cauliflower Wings

Buffalo cauliflower wings are a delicious vegetarian alternative to the fatty wings served at your local dive bar. These cauliflower hot wings are spicy, and they give you the option of controlling the spice level based on what buffalo sauce you choose. It's a great healthier way to enjoy hot wings without the fat and calories! Serve with ranch dressing.

Hands-On Time: 5 minutes
Cook Time: 12 minutes

Serves 1

¼ head cauliflower, cut into florets
¼ cup buffalo sauce
½ cup panko bread crumbs

1 In a medium bowl, toss cauliflower in buffalo sauce.

2 Place panko in a gallon-sized plastic zip-top bag. Using tongs, move cauliflower from bowl into bag and toss to coat. Place coated bites in air fryer basket and spritz with olive oil spray. Air fry at 400°F for 8 minutes.

3 Open air fryer and gently turn cauliflower, being careful not to loosen coating. Spritz again with olive oil spray. Lower temperature to 350°F and air fry 4 minutes more.

4 Using tongs, remove from air fryer and serve.

PER SERVING

CALORIES: 139 | FAT: 1g | SODIUM: 1,921mg | CARBOHYDRATES: 28g | FIBER: 1g | SUGAR: 2g | PROTEIN: 5g

Extra-Crispy Fried Pickles

Fried pickles are one of the most famous restaurant appetizers, but can you make them in the air fryer? This recipe proves that the answer is a resounding yes! They are just as crunchy but have the healthy benefit of not being deep-fried. Crunchier than their deep-fried cousins, these little gems are irresistible and perfect with ranch dressing.

Hands-On Time: 10 minutes
Cook Time: 8 minutes

Serves 1

⅓ cup all-purpose flour
1 large egg, beaten
⅓ cup panko bread crumbs
15 pickle chips

1 Prepare breading station with three medium dishes. Place flour in the first dish, beaten egg in the second dish, and panko in the third dish.

2 Remove pickle chips from jar and place individually into flour. Dredge chips in flour on both sides. Next, dip chips in egg on both sides so all flour is coated. Then dredge chips in panko.

3 Place chips on a cutting board and spritz on one side with olive oil spray. Place chips sprayed-side down in air fryer basket. Air fry at 400°F for 4 minutes.

4 Open air fryer, flip chips, and spritz again with olive oil spray. Air fry 4 minutes more.

5 Using tongs, remove from air fryer and serve.

PER SERVING

CALORIES: 296 | **FAT:** 6g | **SODIUM:** 943mg | **CARBOHYDRATES:** 47g | **FIBER:** 2g | **SUGAR:** 2g | **PROTEIN:** 13g

Bacon-Wrapped Taco-Stuffed Jalapeño Poppers

Bacon-wrapped jalapeño poppers will be your new go-to craving! Mix things up by stuffing the jalapeños with a taco-seasoned cream cheese filling. You might want to double the recipe because you'll love them so much. Thick-cut hearty bacon is great for this recipe. If using thin-sliced bacon, reduce the cooking time by 3–5 minutes.

Hands-On Time: 10 minutes
Cook Time: 15 minutes

Serves 1

- **2 ounces full-fat cream cheese**
- **⅓ cup shredded Colby jack cheese**
- **1 tablespoon taco seasoning**
- **2 (4") jalapeño peppers, halved lengthwise with stems intact, seeds and membranes removed**
- **4 strips thick-cut bacon**
- **3 tablespoons barbecue sauce**

SEASONING ADVICE

Not a fan of taco seasoning? Replace it with ranch seasoning mix. Buy these types of seasoning in bulk. That way you can add just the amount you need to any recipe. This is especially helpful when cooking for one!

1 In a medium bowl, using an electric hand mixer on medium speed, mix cream cheese, Colby jack, and taco seasoning. Spoon filling into jalapeño halves. The amount of cream cheese mixture will vary based on jalapeño size.

2 Wrap 1 bacon strip tightly around each jalapeño half. It should spiral around the jalapeño half.

3 Place jalapeños in air fryer basket and lightly baste with barbecue sauce. Air fry at 375°F for 15 minutes until bacon is crispy.

4 Remove from air fryer and let cool slightly before serving.

PER SERVING

CALORIES: 785 | **FAT:** 51g | **SODIUM:** 2,732mg | **CARBOHYDRATES:** 32g | **FIBER:** 2g | **SUGAR:** 21g | **PROTEIN:** 37g

Hot and Crunchy Cream Cheese and Pepper Jelly

Sometimes you're hungry and are craving something a little fun and fancy. But what happens if you don't feel like making a whole meal? This appetizer is sure to satisfy. Keep cream cheese and pepper jelly in the house and you'll always be ready for this snack. Hearty, crispy crackers would be delicious with this appetizer.

Hands-On Time: 5 minutes
Cook Time: 5 minutes

Serves 1

- 2 ounces full-fat cream cheese
- 2 tablespoons all-purpose flour
- 1 large egg, beaten
- ¼ cup panko bread crumbs
- 4 ounces pepper jelly (any flavor)

SUBSTITUTE GOAT CHEESE

Goat cheese is a delicious soft cheese! It comes in a small log and is the perfect size for this appetizer. It's a little tangier than cream cheese but works well as an alternative. Plus, you can find cranberry or blueberry goat cheese, which makes this dish more festive.

1 Place cream cheese in the freezer for 20 minutes.

2 Prepare breading station with three medium dishes. Place flour in the first dish, egg in the second dish, and panko in the third dish.

3 Remove cream cheese from the freezer. Roll in flour, coating all sides. Next, dip in egg, making sure all flour is coated. Finally, roll cream cheese in panko, pressing panko into all sides.

4 Using tongs, place cream cheese in air fryer basket. Spritz with olive oil spray. Air fry at 375°F for 5 minutes.

5 Remove cream cheese from the air fryer and set on a small plate. Spoon pepper jelly over cream cheese. Serve.

PER SERVING

CALORIES: 600 | **FAT:** 20g | **SODIUM:** 436mg | **CARBOHYDRATES:** 92g | **FIBER:** 0g | **SUGAR:** 71g | **PROTEIN:** 10g

Bacon-Wrapped Jalapeño Popper Shrimp

These bacon-wrapped shrimp are stuffed with jalapeños and cream cheese, but don't stop there! Top them with a little barbecue sauce for an extra sweet and spicy zing. These tasty shrimp bites are a fun little appetizer that you'll gobble up in minutes. If using a thicker cut of bacon, you will need to add 3–4 minutes of cook time.

Hands-On Time: 10 minutes

Cook Time: 12 minutes

Serves 1

- 5 raw jumbo shrimp, peeled and deveined
- 3 strips thin-sliced bacon, cut in half
- 2½ teaspoons full-fat cream cheese, divided
- ½ medium jalapeño pepper, trimmed, seeds and membranes removed, thinly sliced
- 2 tablespoons barbecue sauce

NAAN OR PITA ROUNDS

Sometimes when you cook bacon in the air fryer, the grease can cause your air fryer to smoke. If you put bread under the tray to catch the drippings, it prevents smoking. In this recipe, if you use mini naan or pita rounds to catch the drippings, you can eat the savory bread with your meal.

1 Using a sharp, thin knife, butterfly shrimp. Do this by holding the shrimp by the tail and cutting along the outer curve of the shrimp so that it opens up like a folder. Be careful not to slice all the way through. Thick end of each shrimp should open.

2 Using a small spoon, smear ½ teaspoon cream cheese into opening of each shrimp. Add 1 thin slice jalapeño to the opening of each shrimp. Tightly wrap 1 piece bacon around each shrimp. Place wrapped shrimp on a small plate and refrigerate 15 minutes.

3 Remove shrimp from refrigerator and, using tongs, place shrimp in air fryer basket. Lightly baste with barbecue sauce. Air fry at 350°F for 6 minutes.

4 Open air fryer, flip shrimp, and baste again. Air fry 6 minutes more.

5 Using tongs, carefully remove shrimp from air fryer and serve.

PER SERVING

CALORIES: 258 | FAT: 13g | SODIUM: 1,105mg | CARBOHYDRATES: 15g | FIBER: 1g | SUGAR: 12g | PROTEIN: 17g

Grilled Cheese Roll-Ups

Looking to put a spin on a childhood favorite? These roll-ups are a super-quick version. Plus, since they're rolled up, they're ready-made to dip into ranch dressing or tomato soup.

Hands-On Time: 5 minutes
Cook Time: 5 minutes

Serves 1

2 (¾"-thick) slices white bread
1 tablespoon salted butter, softened
2 (1-ounce) slices American cheese

1 Lay bread slices on a cutting board. With a rolling pin, flatten bread slices.

2 Spread butter on top of bread slices. Lay cheese on buttered side of bread slices. Tightly roll bread and cheese together.

3 Open air fryer and lightly spray tray with nonstick cooking spray. Place rolls in air fryer and spritz with olive oil spray. Air fry at 350°F for 5 minutes.

4 Using tongs, carefully remove rolls and serve.

PER SERVING

CALORIES: 422 | **FAT:** 20g | **SODIUM:** 1,196mg | **CARBOHYDRATES:** 41g | **FIBER:** 2g | **SUGAR:** 8g | **PROTEIN:** 16g

Garlic Bread

Garlic Bread is simple and affordable, and it's ready in less than 10 minutes. This recipe also has a secret ingredient that everybody will love. Air fryer garlic bread pairs perfectly with the Chicken Parmesan in Chapter 5 or Shrimp Scampi in Chapter 7.

Hands-On Time: 5 minutes
Cook Time: 4 minutes

Serves 1

2 tablespoons salted butter, softened
¼ teaspoon ranch seasoning mix
¼ teaspoon Italian seasoning
½ teaspoon minced garlic
2 (1"-thick) slices Italian bread

1 Place butter in a small bowl and mix in ranch seasoning, Italian seasoning, and garlic. Spread a thick coating of garlic butter on top of each piece of bread.

2 Place bread slices buttered-side up in air fryer. Air fry at 350°F for 4–5 minutes.

3 Remove from air fryer and serve.

PER SERVING

CALORIES: 369 | **FAT:** 23g | **SODIUM:** 616mg | **CARBOHYDRATES:** 31g | **FIBER:** 2g | **SUGAR:** 1g | **PROTEIN:** 6g

Candied Pecans

Candied pecans are a festival staple, but what about when it's not festival season? You can make these crunchy, sugary delights in your own kitchen. Substitute walnuts or cashews for the pecans if you prefer. These pecans are best served warm, just like you get them at the fair.

Hands-On Time: 5 minutes
Cook Time: 6 minutes

Serves 1

- **2 tablespoons granulated sugar**
- **2 tablespoons light brown sugar**
- **½ teaspoon ground cinnamon**
- **⅟₁₆ teaspoon salt**
- **2 tablespoons salted butter, melted**
- **½ teaspoon vanilla extract**
- **½ cup pecans**

1 In a medium bowl, mix both sugars, cinnamon, and salt. In another medium bowl, whisk together butter and vanilla. Add pecans to butter mixture and toss to coat.

2 Add coated pecans and any remaining butter mixture to sugar mixture and toss until pecans are well coated.

3 Line air fryer basket with parchment paper. Spoon coated pecans onto parchment in a single layer. Spoon any excess sugar mixture onto pecans as well. Air fry at 350°F for 3 minutes. Open air fryer and stir pecans, then air fry 3 minutes more.

4 Remove parchment with pecans from air fryer and let cool 10 minutes. Break apart any pieces that are stuck together and serve.

PER SERVING

CALORIES: 754 | FAT: 55g | SODIUM: 334mg | CARBOHYDRATES: 60g | FIBER: 5g | SUGAR: 54g | PROTEIN: 5g

Buffalo Ranch Snack Mix

This snack mix is a perfect movie night treat, and you can put it together in just a few minutes. Get a movie picked out and prep your snack mix. Pop it in the air fryer and get started on the movie. When you're ready for a break, the snack mix will be ready for you. This spicy ranch version will have you wanting more.

Hands-On Time: 5 minutes
Cook Time: 10 minutes

Serves 1

- 1 tablespoon salted butter, melted
- ½ tablespoon Worcestershire sauce
- ¼ teaspoon salt
- 1 tablespoon buffalo sauce
- 1 teaspoon ranch seasoning mix
- ¾ cup Honey Nut Chex cereal
- 2 tablespoons salted peanuts
- 2 tablespoons mini pretzel sticks

1 In a large bowl, whisk together butter, Worcestershire sauce, salt, buffalo sauce, and ranch seasoning. Add Chex, peanuts, and pretzels to butter mixture and toss to coat.

2 Spread Chex mixture into a single layer in air fryer basket. Air fry at 270°F for 5 minutes.

3 Open air fryer and shake basket to lightly toss snack mix. Lower temperature to 250°F and air fry 5 minutes more.

4 Pour snack mix from air fryer into a large bowl. Let cool completely, 10–15 minutes. Store in a zip-top bag or an airtight container until snack time!

PER SERVING

CALORIES: 401 | **FAT:** 21g | **SODIUM:** 2,005mg | **CARBOHYDRATES:** 47g | **FIBER:** 3g | **SUGAR:** 12g | **PROTEIN:** 8g

Beef Jerky

Beef jerky is a delicious and nutritious snack. Did you know you can use your air fryer to make a homemade version? Thinly sliced lean cuts of beef work best for this recipe. The rest of the ingredients are likely already in your pantry. It's a great snack to pop in a bag and keep in your car when you're on the go.

Hands-On Time: 5 minutes
Cook Time: 60 minutes

Serves 1

1 (8-ounce) eye of round steak
2 tablespoons light brown sugar
2 tablespoons soy sauce
2 tablespoons Worcestershire sauce
½ teaspoon minced garlic
⅛ teaspoon red pepper flakes
⅛ teaspoon liquid smoke

1 On a cutting board, tenderize steak with a meat tenderizer. Slice steak against the grain into 1½"-wide slices, about ¼" thick.

2 In a gallon-sized plastic zip-top bag, combine all remaining ingredients. Seal bag and shake to combine.

3 Add steak slices to bag and reseal. Be sure all slices are completely coated in marinade. Marinate in refrigerator at least 2 hours.

4 Remove steak from bag and discard marinade. Place steak in air fryer basket in a single layer. Air fry at 180°F for 60 minutes.

5 Remove jerky from air fryer and let cool. Store in a zip-top bag until ready to serve.

PER SERVING

CALORIES: 331 | **FAT:** 7g | **SODIUM:** 330mg | **CARBOHYDRATES:** 4g | **FIBER:** 0g | **SUGAR:** 3g | **PROTEIN:** 56g

Bacon-Wrapped Mini Sausages

Slow cooker mini smoked sausages are a classic recipe, but they are typically made in a huge batch and swimming in sauce. This updated version is just as tasty but quicker and easier because of your air fryer! The meaty goodness of the sausages is surrounded by savory bacon and a sweet sprinkle of seasoning. No mess and much quicker!

Hands-On Time: 10 minutes
Cook Time: 8 minutes

Serves 1

3 strips bacon, cut into thirds
8 mini smoked sausage links (2 ounces total)
2 tablespoons barbecue sauce
1 tablespoon barbecue seasoning

1 Wrap each piece of bacon around 1 mini sausage and secure with a toothpick.

2 Baste each sausage on both sides with barbecue sauce, then sprinkle with barbecue seasoning. Place bacon-wrapped sausages in a single layer in air fryer basket. Air fry at 375°F for 4 minutes.

3 Open air fryer and flip all sausages, then air fry 4 minutes more.

4 Remove from air fryer and serve.

PER SERVING

CALORIES: 357 | FAT: 23g | SODIUM: 2,434mg | CARBOHYDRATES: 15g | FIBER: 0g | SUGAR: 12g | PROTEIN: 18g

Chicken Philly Taquitos

These Chicken Philly Taquitos are just as fun to make as they are to eat. A thin slice of chicken breast, sweet pepper, and onion rolled up in a tortilla and held together with provolone cheese. A little crunch, a little meat, and a lot of cheese make these a snack you'll love! Serve with some salsa and sour cream to enhance the flavor.

Hands-On Time: 5 minutes
Cook Time: 12 minutes

Serves 1

1 teaspoon olive oil
½ teaspoon taco seasoning
½ (4-ounce) chicken breast, sliced ½" thick
1 mini sweet pepper, sliced ¼" thick
1 (¼"-thick) slice white onion, halved, rings separated
2 (6") low-carb flour tortillas
1 (1-ounce) slice provolone cheese, cut into thin strips

1 Combine oil and taco seasoning in a large bowl. Add chicken, pepper, and onion and toss until combined. Place chicken and vegetables in air fryer basket. Air fry at 375°F for 7 minutes, then remove from air fryer basket.

2 Lay tortillas on a large plate. Divide chicken breast, pepper, onion, and provolone evenly between tortillas.

3 Roll tortillas as tightly as possible. Place seam-side down in air fryer and spritz with olive oil spray. Air fry at 350°F for 3 minutes.

4 Open air fryer, flip taquitos, and spritz again with olive oil spray. Air fry 2 minutes more.

5 Remove from air fryer and serve.

PER SERVING

CALORIES: 370 | **FAT:** 18g | **SODIUM:** 873mg | **CARBOHYDRATES:** 37g | **FIBER:** 19g | **SUGAR:** 4g | **PROTEIN:** 31g

Margherita Flatbread Pizza

Margherita pizza is a classic Italian dish. By using mini naan, you can have a personal pizza any time you like! Pair this pizza with a side salad for a full dinner. Margherita pizza is vegetarian, but you could easily add a few slices of pepperoni if you like.

Hands-On Time: 3 minutes
Cook Time: 6 minutes

Serves 1

- 1 (50-gram) mini garlic naan bread
- 1 tablespoon olive oil
- 1 medium Roma tomato, thinly sliced
- 3 ounces fresh mozzarella cheese, thinly sliced
- 3 fresh basil leaves
- 1⁄16 teaspoon coarse sea salt

1. On a cutting board, lay out naan and baste one side with oil. Top with tomato, mozzarella, basil, and salt.

2. Carefully place naan in air fryer basket. Air fry at 375°F for 6 minutes.

3. Remove from air fryer and serve.

PER SERVING

CALORIES: 457 | **FAT:** 28g | **SODIUM:** 506mg | **CARBOHYDRATES:** 31g | **FIBER:** 2g | **SUGAR:** 6g | **PROTEIN:** 18g

TRY IT WITH TORTILLAS

If you can't find mini naan bread in your grocery store, you can use flour tortillas in this recipe instead. Tortillas, especially the low-carb ones, are a perfect healthy option for a pizza crust! If you're missing the garlic flavor, add ¼ teaspoon of minced garlic.

Crispy Breaded Shrimp

Are the small popcorn shrimp served at every restaurant not cutting it? Try this satisfying and hearty appetizer with a few large shrimp instead! Sprinkle with juice from a fresh lemon and dip in cocktail sauce for a restaurant treat in your own kitchen.

Hands-On Time: 8 minutes
Cook Time: 8 minutes

Serves 1

- 2 tablespoons all-purpose flour
- 1 tablespoon Old Bay Seasoning
- 1 large egg, beaten
- ¼ cup panko bread crumbs
- 5 raw jumbo shrimp, peeled and deveined

1 Prepare breading station with three medium dishes. Mix flour and Old Bay Seasoning with a fork in the first dish, place beaten egg in the second dish, and spread panko in the third dish. Holding shrimp by tail, dredge in flour mixture, then dip in egg, making sure all flour is coated. Finally, dredge in panko, pressing on the outside to help it stick.

2 Lay shrimp in air fryer tray and spritz with olive oil spray. Air fry at 350°F for 4 minutes. Open air fryer, flip shrimp, and spritz again with olive oil spray.

3 Air fry 4 minutes more. Remove from air fryer and serve.

PER SERVING

CALORIES: 223 | **FAT:** 4g | **SODIUM:** 851mg | **CARBOHYDRATES:** 27g | **FIBER:** 0g | **SUGAR:** 1g | **PROTEIN:** 19g

Potato Chips

Potato chips are the number one snack food, but they're typically greasy and full of preservatives! Making your own from scratch is simple and tastier. These chips are reminiscent of the spiral-cut fries at the state fair! Plus, you can whip up a fry sauce for dipping while they are cooking.

Hands-On Time: 5 minutes
Cook Time: 11 minutes

Serves 1

Chips
1 small russet potato, scrubbed clean
2 cups ice water
½ teaspoon coarse sea salt, divided

Dipping Sauce
1 tablespoon ketchup
1 tablespoon mayonnaise

1 To make Chips: Using a mandoline, carefully slice potato ⅛" thick. Place slices in a large bowl of ice water and soak for 30 minutes. Drain potatoes and pat dry with a clean kitchen towel.

2 Line air fryer basket with parchment paper. Place potato slices in a single layer in air fryer basket so they do not overlap. More than one batch may be required. Spritz with olive oil spray and sprinkle with ¼ teaspoon salt. Air fry at 370°F for 7 minutes.

3 Open air fryer and flip slices. Spritz again with olive oil spray and sprinkle with remaining ¼ teaspoon salt. Air fry 4 minutes more. After 2 minutes, try Chips to see if they are done to your liking.

4 To make Dipping Sauce: In a small bowl, mix ketchup and mayonnaise.

5 Remove Chips from air fryer and serve with Dipping Sauce.

PER SERVING

CALORIES: 243 | FAT: 10g | SODIUM: 1,220mg | CARBOHYDRATES: 34g | FIBER: 3g | SUGAR: 5g | PROTEIN: 4g

Sides

When you go out to eat, sometimes the sides that come with a main dish are the reason you put the order through. When you're in the mood for fries, a side salad just isn't going to cut it. Here's some good news: Because of your air fryer, you can cook up any number of sides to go with your main meal, as long as you have the ingredients! The best part: You'll likely save time and money by doing it yourself.

This chapter covers all your favorite vegetable and potato side dishes and will probably give you a few new ones you might not have thought of before! Frequent favorites like Crispy Brussels Sprouts and Twice-Baked Potatoes will definitely keep your cravings at bay. And if you want to try something new and delicious, cook up some Carrot Fries, Spicy Breaded Okra Nuggets, or Cabbage Steaks.

Breaded Mushrooms

Breaded mushrooms are a restaurant favorite and go with everything from burgers to pasta. With the air fryer, there's no mess and no oil! Even without the oil, they are still crunchy and delicious. Serve with ranch dressing.

Hands-On Time: 10 minutes
Cook Time: 12 minutes

Serves 1

¼ cup all-purpose flour
¼ teaspoon salt
¼ teaspoon ground black
  pepper
½ teaspoon garlic powder
1 large egg
⅛ teaspoon hot sauce
¼ cup panko bread crumbs
5 button mushrooms

1 Prepare breading station with three medium dishes. In the first dish, mix flour, salt, pepper, and garlic powder with a fork. In the second dish, beat together egg and hot sauce. In the third dish, spread panko.

2 Bread mushrooms by dipping them into flour, then egg, and then panko, coating all sides.

3 Place mushrooms in air fryer at least 1" apart. Spritz mushrooms with olive oil spray. Air fry at 370°F for 6 minutes. Open air fryer, turn mushrooms, and spritz again with olive oil spray. Air fry 6 minutes more.

4 Remove from air fryer and serve.

PER SERVING

CALORIES: 212 | **FAT:** 3g | **SODIUM:** 403mg | **CARBOHYDRATES:** 36g | **FIBER:** 1g | **SUGAR:** 3g | **PROTEIN:** 11g

Four-Ingredient Air Fryer–Roasted Cauliflower

Roasted cauliflower is a savory, popular side. Plus, it's quick and easy to make in the air fryer!

Hands-On Time: 3 minutes
Cook Time: 17 minutes

Serves 1

1½ cups fresh cauliflower florets
¼ cup light Italian dressing
1 tablespoon freshly grated Parmesan cheese
⅛ teaspoon salt

1 Toss cauliflower florets in dressing. Place florets in air fryer basket. Air fry at 400°F for 10 minutes.

2 Open air fryer and shake to lightly toss florets. Sprinkle Parmesan over cauliflower. Air fry 7 minutes more.

3 Remove cauliflower from air fryer and sprinkle with salt. Serve.

PER SERVING

CALORIES: 202 | FAT: 13g | SODIUM: 1,011mg | CARBOHYDRATES: 16g | FIBER: 3g | SUGAR: 9g | PROTEIN: 5g

Cabbage Steaks

Air fryer Cabbage Steaks are one of the healthiest side dishes you can make! Best of all, they're done in 15 minutes. This dish has only three ingredients and is perfect to serve alongside the Marinated Chicken Breast in Chapter 5.

Hands-On Time: 5 minutes
Cook Time: 10 minutes

Serves 1

¼ head cabbage, sliced 1½" thick
1 tablespoon Greek salad dressing, divided
1⁄16 teaspoon coarse sea salt, divided

1 Place cabbage slices in air fryer in a single layer. Brush with half of dressing and sprinkle with half of salt. Air fry at 375°F for 5 minutes.

2 Open air fryer, flip steaks, brush with remaining dressing, and sprinkle with remaining salt. Air fry 5 minutes more.

3 Remove from air fryer and serve.

PER SERVING

CALORIES: 91 | FAT: 3g | SODIUM: 305mg | CARBOHYDRATES: 15g | FIBER: 6g | SUGAR: 9g | PROTEIN: 3g

Spicy Zucchini Fries

Zucchini fries are such a delicious side dish to serve with any meal! You'll be amazed at how crunchy and delicious they are. Zucchini is such a versatile vegetable, and when you're looking for a new way to serve it, this is a great easy option.

Hands-On Time: 10 minutes
Cook Time: 8 minutes

Serves 1

½ medium zucchini
½ cup hot wing breading flour
1 large egg
1 tablespoon hot sauce
½ cup panko bread crumbs
½ tablespoon coarse sea salt
1 lime wedge

SPICY RANCH DRESSING

You can make up a quick spicy ranch dressing by mixing ranch dressing and buffalo sauce in a 3:1 ratio, or according to your preferred spice level! This is a delicious sauce to serve with these fries.

1 Slice zucchini half in half lengthwise, then slice each half into 4 wedges, yielding 8 zucchini wedges.

2 Prepare breading station with three medium dishes. In the first dish, spread out hot wing breading flour. In the second dish, beat together egg and hot sauce. In the third dish, spread panko and mix in salt. Using a fork, dip zucchini wedges into flour, then egg mixture, and then panko, coating all sides.

3 Place wedges in air fryer at least 1" apart. Spritz with olive oil spray. Air fry at 400°F for 4 minutes. Open air fryer, flip wedges, and spritz again with olive oil spray. Air fry 4 minutes more.

4 Remove zucchini fries from air fryer and squeeze juice from lime wedge over them. Serve.

PER SERVING

CALORIES: 211 | FAT: 3g | SODIUM: 2,502mg | CARBOHYDRATES: 35g | FIBER: 1g | SUGAR: 4g | PROTEIN: 9g

Potato Pancakes

Air fryer Potato Pancakes are a delicious and unique side dish. They're also a great way to use up leftovers. This recipe transforms mashed potatoes into a crispy and cheesy new dish. You can use your favorite cheese in place of white Cheddar.

Hands-On Time: 10 minutes
Cook Time: 10 minutes

Serves 1

⅓ cup chilled leftover mashed potatoes
1 tablespoon all-purpose flour
2 tablespoons shredded sharp white Cheddar cheese
1 tablespoon dried chives
½ teaspoon minced garlic
¼ teaspoon plus ¹⁄₁₆ teaspoon salt, divided
¼ cup panko bread crumbs
2 teaspoons sour cream
½ teaspoon chopped fresh chives

1 In a medium bowl, mix potatoes, flour, Cheddar, dried chives, garlic, and ¼ teaspoon salt. Spread panko on a large plate. Spoon half of potato mixture into your hand and lightly form into a ball. Repeat with remaining potato mixture. Lightly flatten each ball into a patty.

2 Lay 1 patty in panko and pat breading onto both sides of patty. Repeat with second patty. Place coated patties on a medium plate and freeze 10–15 minutes.

3 Remove plate from freezer. Spray tray in air fryer basket with nonstick cooking spray. Carefully place patties in air fryer and spritz with olive oil spray. Air fry at 400°F for 5 minutes.

4 Open air fryer. Using a thin metal spatula, flip pancakes. Spritz again with olive oil spray and sprinkle with remaining ¹⁄₁₆ teaspoon salt. Air fry 5 minutes more.

5 Remove pancakes from air fryer and serve with sour cream and fresh chives.

PER SERVING

CALORIES: 284 | **FAT:** 10g | **SODIUM:** 1,096mg | **CARBOHYDRATES:** 39g | **FIBER:** 1g | **SUGAR:** 2g | **PROTEIN:** 9g

Carrot Fries

Roasted carrots are great, but they take time—that is, unless you're making them in your air fryer! These Carrot Fries are great when paired with the Breaded Pork Loin Sandwich in Chapter 6 or the Buffalo Cheddar Crispy Chicken in Chapter 5. This recipe was inspired by a quick-serve burger chain. Serve with a side of ranch dressing for dipping.

Hands-On Time: 5 minutes
Cook Time: 15 minutes

Serves 1

1 medium carrot, peeled and
    cut into sticks
1 tablespoon olive oil
1 tablespoon lemon herb
    seasoning

1 Place carrot sticks in a medium bowl and add oil and seasoning. Toss carrots until coated.

2 Place carrot fries in air fryer in a single layer. Air fry at 350°F for 8 minutes.

3 Open air fryer and shake fries. Air fry 7 minutes more.

4 Remove from air fryer and serve.

PER SERVING

CALORIES: 144 | **FAT:** 13g | **SODIUM:** 2,322mg | **CARBOHYDRATES:** 6g | **FIBER:** 2g | **SUGAR:** 3g | **PROTEIN:** 1g

Roasted Asparagus

Air fryer asparagus is a family favorite side dish! You don't need anything but the vegetable, sea salt, and your air fryer, and it's delicious every time! The real bonus is that it's ready in just 10 minutes. This side dish is a perfect accompaniment to nearly any main dish, and you can cook the dishes together to save time.

Hands-On Time: 3 minutes
Cook Time: 7 minutes

Serves 1

½ pound asparagus, ends
    trimmed
¹⁄₁₆ teaspoon coarse sea salt

1 Snap asparagus spears in half if necessary to fit into your air fryer. Place asparagus in air fryer in a single layer. Spritz with olive oil spray and sprinkle with salt. Air fry at 350°F for 4 minutes.

2 Open air fryer. Using tongs, flip asparagus and spritz again with olive oil spray. Air fry 3 minutes more. If asparagus is very thin, you may need to air fry for only 5 minutes total.

3 Remove from air fryer and serve.

PER SERVING

CALORIES: 31 | FAT: 0g | SODIUM: 123mg | CARBOHYDRATES: 6g | FIBER: 3g | SUGAR: 3g | PROTEIN: 3g

Jalapeño Fries

Jalapeño fries are going to be your new favorite side dish! Even if you're not a big fan of spicy food, these Jalapeño Fries will be worth challenging your spice tolerance. You remove all the seeds, so you're left with just the yummy, crunchy pepper. Serve with a salsa ranch dressing and enjoy.

Hands-On Time: 10 minutes
Cook Time: 10 minutes

Serves 1

3 (4") jalapeño peppers, trimmed and quartered lengthwise, seeds and membranes removed
½ cup all-purpose flour
1 large egg, beaten
¾ cup panko bread crumbs

SALSA RANCH DRESSING

You can make up a quick salsa ranch dressing by mixing together ranch dressing and salsa in a 2:1 ratio, or according to your preferred spice level! This dressing adds a little spice to any recipe.

1   Rinse jalapeño strips lightly with water so they're damp.

2   Prepare breading station with three medium dishes. Place flour in the first dish, egg in the second dish, and panko in the third dish. Bread jalapeño strips by dipping them into flour, then egg, and then panko, coating all sides.

3   Place jalapeño strips in air fryer at least 1" apart in a single layer. Spritz with olive oil spray. Air fry at 375°F for 5 minutes.

4   Open air fryer, flip jalapeños, and spritz again with olive oil spray. Air fry 5 minutes more.

5   Remove from air fryer and serve.

PER SERVING

CALORIES: 187 | FAT: 4g | SODIUM: 109mg | CARBOHYDRATES: 31g | FIBER: 1g | SUGAR: 3g | PROTEIN: 8g

Spicy Breaded Okra Nuggets

Breaded okra is a staple in the South, but regardless of where you're from, you'll love these nuggets! They pair especially well with ranch dressing. Spicy panko bread crumbs make this even tastier, but if you can't find the spicy kind, regular panko works just fine.

Hands-On Time: 10 minutes
Cook Time: 12 minutes

Serves 1

½ cup all-purpose flour
½ teaspoon cayenne pepper
1 large egg
1 tablespoon water
½ cup spicy panko bread crumbs
5 medium okra, stemmed and cut into 1" chunks

1 Prepare breading station with three medium dishes. In the first dish, mix flour and cayenne pepper. In the second dish, beat egg and water. In the third dish, spread panko. Bread okra by dipping into flour, then egg, and then panko, coating all sides.

2 Add okra chunks to air fryer at least 1" apart in a single layer. Spritz okra with olive oil spray. Air fry at 375°F for 6 minutes.

3 Open air fryer, shake basket to toss okra, and spritz again with olive oil spray. Air fry 6 minutes more.

4 Remove from air fryer and serve.

PER SERVING

CALORIES: 268 | FAT: 3g | SODIUM: 94mg | CARBOHYDRATES: 49g | FIBER: 3g | SUGAR: 2g | PROTEIN: 11g

Cheesy Tomato Slices

Summer's most plentiful fruit is tomatoes, but finding new ways to eat them can be difficult. This recipe jazzes up plain tomatoes in your air fryer by adding a little cheese and fresh basil. They're ready in only 7 minutes!

Hands-On Time: 2 minutes
Cook Time: 5 minutes

Serves 1

1 small tomato
2 fresh basil leaves
1 tablespoon grated
  Parmesan cheese
6 fresh mozzarella pearls
  (2 ounces total)
1⁄16 teaspoon coarse sea salt

1 Slice off ends of tomato and cut remaining tomato into 2 thick slices.

2 Place tomato slices in air fryer. Top each slice with 1 basil leaf, ½ tablespoon Parmesan, and 3 mozzarella pearls. Air fry at 350°F for 5 minutes.

3 Remove from air fryer, sprinkle with salt, and serve.

PER SERVING

CALORIES: 158 | FAT: 9g | SODIUM: 315mg | CARBOHYDRATES: 6g | FIBER: 1g | SUGAR: 4g | PROTEIN: 10g

Crispy Steak House Potato Wedges

Steak house–style potato wedges are crunchy on the outside and fluffy on the inside. Leave the skins on for that steak house flair and they'll be on the table in 25 minutes. These are the perfect side dish for Mom's Meatloaf in Chapter 6.

Hands-On Time: 5 minutes
Cook Time: 20 minutes

Serves 1

1 medium russet potato,
  sliced into 8 wedges
1 tablespoon olive oil
1 teaspoon coarse sea salt

1 Place potato wedges in a large bowl. Add oil and salt and toss to coat wedges. Place wedges in air fryer in a single layer. Air fry at 400°F for 10 minutes.

2 Open air fryer. Using tongs, flip wedges. Air fry 10 minutes more.

3 Remove from air fryer and serve.

PER SERVING

CALORIES: 286 | FAT: 13g | SODIUM: 1,944mg | CARBOHYDRATES: 37g | FIBER: 4g | SUGAR: 2g | PROTEIN: 5g

Fried Green Tomatoes

Fried green tomatoes are a staple in the South. Next time you see these tomatoes at the farmers' market, grab a handful! Fried green tomatoes are firm and refreshing with a light and crunchy coating. The dipping sauce is light and complements the crunchy tomatoes.

Hands-On Time: 10 minutes
Cook Time: 6 minutes

Serves 1

Fried Green Tomatoes
1 medium green tomato
1⁄16 teaspoon salt
1⁄16 teaspoon ground black pepper
¼ cup all-purpose flour
1 teaspoon garlic powder
1 large egg, beaten
½ cup panko bread crumbs
¼ teaspoon cayenne pepper
¼ teaspoon paprika

Dipping Sauce
2 tablespoons buttermilk
2 tablespoons mayonnaise
2 tablespoons barbecue sauce
1 lime wedge
1⁄16 teaspoon salt

HOMEMADE BUTTERMILK

Don't have buttermilk? There's no need to buy a pint when you need just 2 tablespoons! You can make buttermilk with just two ingredients: 2% milk and white vinegar. Simply mix 2 tablespoons milk and ½ teaspoon white vinegar. If you don't have white vinegar, you may substitute ½ teaspoon lemon juice.

1 To make Fried Green Tomatoes: Slice tomato ½" thick and sprinkle with salt and black pepper.

2 Prepare breading station with three medium dishes. Mix flour and garlic powder in the first dish. Place beaten egg in the second dish. Mix panko, cayenne pepper, and paprika in the third dish. Bread tomato slices by dipping them into flour, then egg, and then panko, coating all sides.

3 Place tomato slices in air fryer at least 1" apart in a single layer. Spritz with olive oil spray. Air fry at 375°F for 3 minutes.

4 Open air fryer, flip tomato slices, and spritz again with olive oil spray. Air fry 3 minutes more.

5 To make Dipping Sauce: While tomato slices are cooking, in a small bowl, mix together buttermilk, mayonnaise, barbecue sauce, juice from lime wedge, and salt. Cover and refrigerate until ready to serve.

6 Remove tomato slices from air fryer and serve with Dipping Sauce.

PER SERVING

CALORIES: 517 | **FAT:** 27g | **SODIUM:** 1,013mg | **CARBOHYDRATES:** 54g | **FIBER:** 3g | **SUGAR:** 22g | **PROTEIN:** 14g

Super-Crunchy Onion Rings

Making air fryer onion rings from scratch is so easy! Cut, dip, air fry. These onion rings are extra-crunchy perfection, and you can make a quick dipping sauce to go with them!

Hands-On Time: 10 minutes
Cook Time: 10 minutes

Serves 1

Onion Rings
½ small yellow onion, ends sliced off, peeled, and cut into 2 (¾") slices
½ cup all-purpose flour
1 teaspoon seasoning salt
1 large egg, beaten
½ cup panko bread crumbs
½ teaspoon coarse sea salt

Dipping Sauce
2 tablespoons mayonnaise
2 tablespoons ketchup
1 teaspoon seasoning salt

1 To make Onion Rings: Separate onion into individual rings.

2 Prepare breading station with three medium dishes. Mix flour and seasoning salt in the first dish. Place beaten egg in the second dish. Mix panko and sea salt in the third dish. Bread Onion Rings by dipping into flour, then egg, and then panko, coating all sides.

3 Add Onion Rings to air fryer in a single layer. Spritz Onion Rings with olive oil spray. Air fry at 375°F for 10 minutes.

4 To make Dipping Sauce: Mix all ingredients well.

5 Remove Onion Rings from air fryer and serve with Dipping Sauce.

PER SERVING

CALORIES: 267 | FAT: 22g | SODIUM: 3,279mg | CARBOHYDRATES: 12g | FIBER: 0g | SUGAR: 8g | PROTEIN: 4g

Jalapeño Cheddar Avocado Fries

Avocado fries are a unique side dish and a great way to use up ripe avocados. The best thing about these is that the dipping sauce is in the fry! Mixing up a quick sour cream dip and using it to coat your avocado fries adds so much flavor.

Hands-On Time: 10 minutes
Cook Time: 10 minutes

Serves 1

- 1 medium avocado, halved, pitted, and peeled
- ⅓ cup sour cream
- 2 tablespoons shredded Cheddar cheese
- 1 (4") jalapeño pepper, fully grated
- 1 cup panko bread crumbs
- 2 tablespoons chopped fresh cilantro
- ½ medium lime
- 1⁄16 teaspoon coarse sea salt

SOUR CREAM DIP SHORTCUT

If you have a sour cream dip, such as French onion, in your fridge, you can substitute that in this recipe. Just use it in place of the sour cream, Cheddar, and jalapeño!

1 Slice each avocado half into 4 wedges.

2 Prepare breading station with two medium dishes. In the first dish, mix sour cream, Cheddar, and jalapeño. In the second dish, mix panko and cilantro.

3 Dunk avocado wedges in sour cream mixture until fully coated. Using a fork, transfer avocado to second dish and coat all sides with panko.

4 Place coated wedges in air fryer in a single layer. Spritz wedges with olive oil spray. Air fry at 400°F for 5 minutes.

5 Open air fryer, flip all wedges, and spritz again with olive oil spray. Air fry 5 minutes more.

6 Transfer avocado wedges to a small plate. Squeeze lime half over wedges and sprinkle with salt. Serve.

PER SERVING

CALORIES: 735 | FAT! 39g | SODIUM: 421mg | CARBOHYDRATES: 75g | FIBER: 10g | SUGAR: 6g | PROTEIN: 17g

"Baked" Sweet Potato

Sweet potatoes can satisfy a sweet, starchy craving, but it's not very convenient to have to wait an hour for a potato to bake. The air fryer will bake that potato in less than half the time!

Hands-On Time: 2 minutes
Cook Time: 25 minutes

Serves 1

- 1 small sweet potato, scrubbed clean
- 1 teaspoon olive oil
- 1 tablespoon salted butter
- 1 tablespoon light brown sugar

1 Poke potato with a paring knife in a few spots. Rub outside of potato with oil. Place potato in air fryer. Air fry at 400°F for 25 minutes.

2 Open air fryer and check potato for doneness—a paring knife should slide in easily. If needed, air fry 5 minutes more.

3 Remove from air fryer and slice open. Top with butter and sugar and serve.

PER SERVING

CALORIES: 275 | FAT: 15g | SODIUM: 147mg | CARBOHYDRATES: 33g | FIBER: 3g | SUGAR: 17g | PROTEIN: 2g

Crispy Brussels Sprouts

Air frying brussels sprouts is just as good as oven roasting but so much quicker. Be sure not to remove the leaves that separate from the sprout—they get crispy and delicious.

Hands-On Time: 5 minutes
Cook Time: 10 minutes

Serves 1

- 2 tablespoons olive oil
- 2 tablespoons balsamic vinegar
- 1 tablespoon Worcestershire sauce
- ½ teaspoon plus 1⁄16 teaspoon coarse sea salt, divided
- 1 teaspoon ground black pepper
- ½ pound Brussels sprouts, trimmed and quartered

1 In a large bowl, whisk together oil, vinegar, Worcestershire sauce, ½ teaspoon salt, and pepper. Toss Brussels sprouts in oil mixture.

2 Place Brussels sprouts in air fryer basket. Air fry at 350°F for 5 minutes.

3 Open air fryer and shake basket to toss Brussels sprouts. Air fry 5 minutes more.

4 Remove Brussels sprouts from air fryer, sprinkle with remaining 1⁄16 teaspoon salt, and serve.

PER SERVING

CALORIES: 356 | FAT: 27g | SODIUM: 1,294mg | CARBOHYDRATES: 25g | FIBER: 7g | SUGAR: 10g | PROTEIN: 6g

Crispy Kale Chips

Kale chips are so nutritious and have a delicious crunch. They're great as a side for the Santa Fe Chicken Wrap in Chapter 5. These kale chips have all the salty crunch of potato chips with just a touch of oil. You won't even realize you're eating something green!

Hands-On Time: 5 minutes
Cook Time: 14 minutes

Serves 1

½ **pound curly kale, washed**
4 teaspoons soy sauce
2 tablespoons grated
    Parmesan cheese
2 teaspoons olive oil

1 Tear off ribs of kale into pieces and place in a medium bowl.

2 In a small bowl, whisk together soy sauce, Parmesan, and oil. Pour sauce over kale and toss until coated.

3 Place kale in air fryer basket in a single layer—some overlapping is okay, but the air needs to circulate around them. Air fry at 200°F for 10 minutes.

4 Open air fryer and flip kale chips. Air fry 4 minutes more.

5 Remove from air fryer and serve.

PER SERVING

CALORIES: 220 | **FAT:** 12g | **SODIUM:** 1,412mg | **CARBOHYDRATES:** 18g | **FIBER:** 7g | **SUGAR:** 4g | **PROTEIN:** 12g

Dijon Parmesan Potatoes

This recipe takes potatoes and transforms them into an easy, unique, and delicious side dish. Baby potatoes are sliced in half and dipped in Dijon mustard and freshly grated Parmesan cheese. Then, stick them in the air fryer and voilà! The perfect side dish. These pair well with the Chicken Cordon Bleu in Chapter 5 or the Ham Steak in Chapter 6. If you're using medium potatoes, you'll need to add 3–5 minutes to the cook time.

Hands-On Time: 5 minutes
Cook Time: 12 minutes

Serves 1

- **5 small baby red potatoes, halved**
- **2 teaspoons olive oil**
- **1 teaspoon coarse sea salt**
- **1 teaspoon ground black pepper**
- **2 tablespoons Dijon mustard**
- **3 tablespoons grated Parmesan cheese**

FRESH PARMESAN CHEESE

It's easy to grab the pre-grated Parmesan cheese, but this is one ingredient where the convenience is not worth it. Buy a wedge of real Parmesan (or Romano) cheese and grate it fresh on the small side of the grater. You'll experience so much more flavor!

1 Lay potatoes cut-side down on a piece of parchment paper. Drizzle with oil and sprinkle with salt and pepper.

2 Place mustard and Parmesan in separate small bowls. Dip cut side of potato in mustard and be sure it's thickly coated. Dip mustard side in Parmesan.

3 Place potatoes cut-side up in air fryer basket. Air fry at 350°F for 12 minutes. Check potatoes with a sharp knife to see if they are cooked through. Remove from the air fryer and serve.

PER SERVING

CALORIES: 564 | **FAT:** 16g | **SODIUM:** 2,071mg | **CARBOHYDRATES:** 87g | **FIBER:** 9g | **SUGAR:** 7g | **PROTEIN:** 17g

Garlic Mushrooms

Roasted mushrooms are great paired with the Stuffed Pork Chop from Chapter 6. These Garlic Mushrooms are ready in minutes and can even be made at the same time as your entrée for an all-in-one meal!

Hands-On Time: 5 minutes
Cook Time: 8 minutes

Serves 1

- 1 teaspoon olive oil
- 2 teaspoons Worcestershire sauce
- ½ teaspoon minced garlic
- 1/16 teaspoon coarse sea salt
- 1/16 teaspoon ground black pepper
- 4 ounces baby bella mushrooms, halved

1 In a medium bowl, mix oil, Worcestershire sauce, garlic, salt, and pepper. Add mushrooms and toss until coated.

2 Place mushrooms in air fryer basket in a single layer. Air fry at 350°F for 4 minutes. Open air fryer and shake basket to toss mushrooms. Air fry 4 minutes more.

3 Remove from air fryer and serve.

PER SERVING

CALORIES: 73 | FAT: 4g | SODIUM: 238mg | CARBOHYDRATES: 8g | FIBER: 1g | SUGAR: 3g | PROTEIN: 3g

Garlic Herb Artichoke Hearts

If you like, you can use canned artichoke hearts and eliminate the first 4 minutes of cook time.

Hands-On Time: 2 minutes
Cook Time: 8 minutes

Serves 1

- 1 cup frozen quartered artichoke hearts
- 1 teaspoon olive oil
- ½ teaspoon minced garlic
- ¼ teaspoon Italian seasoning
- 1/16 teaspoon coarse sea salt
- 1/16 teaspoon ground black pepper
- ½ medium lemon
- 1 teaspoon freshly grated Parmesan cheese

1 Place artichokes in air fryer basket in a single layer. Air fry at 350°F for 4 minutes.

2 Transfer artichokes to a medium bowl. Add oil, garlic, Italian seasoning, salt, and pepper. Lightly toss artichokes until coated. Pour artichokes back into air fryer. Air fry 4 minutes more.

3 Remove from air fryer. Squeeze lemon half over artichokes and sprinkle with Parmesan. Serve.

PER SERVING

CALORIES: 97 | FAT: 5g | SODIUM: 213mg | CARBOHYDRATES: 11g | FIBER: 5g | SUGAR: 0g | PROTEIN: 4g

Twice-Baked Potatoes

Twice-Baked Potatoes are a delicious comfort food! A light and fluffy baked potato starts the dish. Scoop out part of the potato; mix it with bacon, sour cream, butter, and cheese; and air fry for a fluffy, melty side dish. Twice-Baked Potatoes are perfect with the Ham Steak in Chapter 6.

Hands-On Time: 10 minutes
Cook Time: 33 minutes

Serves 1

- 1 small russet potato, scrubbed clean
- ¼ teaspoon plus ¹⁄₁₆ teaspoon coarse sea salt, divided
- 1 strip bacon
- 2 tablespoons sour cream
- ⅓ cup shredded Cheddar cheese, divided
- ¹⁄₁₆ teaspoon ground black pepper
- 1 tablespoon salted butter, softened
- 1 tablespoon diced green onion

1 Poke potato with a paring knife in a few spots. Spritz outside of potato with olive oil spray and sprinkle with ¼ teaspoon salt. Place potato in air fryer and air fry at 400°F for 20 minutes.

2 Open air fryer and place bacon in air fryer. Close and air fry 8 minutes more.

3 Open air fryer and check potato for doneness—a paring knife should slide in easily. Remove potato and bacon from air fryer and let cool 5 minutes. If potato is not done, air fry 3–5 minutes more. Dice bacon and set aside.

4 In a medium bowl, mix sour cream, half of Cheddar, remaining ¹⁄₁₆ teaspoon salt, and pepper.

5 Slice cooled potato in half and scoop out 80 percent of flesh. Be sure to leave a thin layer of flesh around potato skins. Add scooped potato flesh and butter to sour cream mixture. Mash with fork until combined. Spoon potato mixture into potato skins and top with remaining Cheddar.

6 Return potatoes to air fryer and air fry at 375°F for 5 minutes until cheese is melted.

7 Remove potatoes from air fryer and top with bacon and green onion.

PER SERVING

CALORIES: 476 | FAT: 29g | SODIUM: 1,125mg | CARBOHYDRATES: 31g | FIBER: 3g | SUGAR: 2g | PROTEIN: 17g

No-Yeast Dinner Biscuits

Typically, it's hard to find a recipe that makes a single serving of rolls. However, this recipe is perfect for one person and tastes much better than anything out of a can. These dinner biscuits are so delicious when they're warm and lightly buttered. If you don't have individual silicone baking cups, you can use ramekins.

Hands-On Time: 5 minutes
Cook Time: 10 minutes

Serves 1

½ cup all-purpose flour
½ teaspoon baking powder
½ teaspoon salt
5 tablespoons 2% milk
1 tablespoon mayonnaise

1 Spray two silicone baking cups with nonstick cooking spray.

2 Combine all ingredients in a medium bowl. Batter will be very thick, almost like a dough.

3 Spoon batter into baking cups. Place cups in air fryer and air fry at 325°F for 10 minutes.

4 Remove cups from air fryer and, using pot holders, turn upside down to remove biscuits from cups. Serve.

PER SERVING

CALORIES: 366 | FAT: 13g | SODIUM: 1,525mg | CARBOHYDRATES: 52g | FIBER: 2g | SUGAR: 4g | PROTEIN: 9g

5

Poultry Main Dishes

Poultry, especially chicken, is one of the most important protein sources worldwide. It's a staple in many households because it's quick to cook, very lean, and healthy. That said, because it's so common, chicken can sometimes be boring. That all changes thanks to your air fryer!

This chapter covers unique and new ways to cook chicken, as well as basic techniques that are great any night of the week. You'll find some typical dishes served at restaurants, such as Chinese Restaurant Chicken on a Stick and Garlic Parmesan Chicken Wings. Looking for something to throw together midday? There are recipes for lunchtime specialties like a Chicken Popper Wrap and a Chicken Teriyaki Sandwich. Or, if you're needing a pick-me-up, there are elegant dinner ideas such as Chicken Cordon Bleu and Apple and Sage Turkey Breast.

Chinese Restaurant Chicken on a Stick

Chicken on a stick at the Chinese buffet is always a favorite. You can make this chicken teriyaki at home—it's so simple and just as delicious! These chicken skewers are made with chicken thighs, which are one of the most tender cuts of chicken.

Hands-On Time: 5 minutes
Cook Time: 12 minutes

Serves 1

2 (3-ounce) boneless, skinless chicken thighs, cut lengthwise into thirds
½ cup teriyaki sauce

SECRET OF THE PINK CHICKEN

When you get chicken on a stick in a Chinese restaurant, it's usually very pink. Here's the simple secret: red food coloring! You can add beet juice in place of food coloring if you really want that pink color.

1 Place chicken in a gallon-sized plastic zip-top bag. Add teriyaki sauce to bag and toss chicken until coated. Seal bag and marinate in refrigerator at least 1 hour, preferably overnight.

2 Using 6" wood skewers, skewer chicken. Place in air fryer basket and air fry at 350°F for 6 minutes.

3 Open air fryer and flip chicken skewers. Air fry 6 minutes more.

4 Remove from air fryer and serve.

PER SERVING

CALORIES: 331 | FAT: 12g | SODIUM: 1,509mg | CARBOHYDRATES: 6g | FIBER: 0g | SUGAR: 5g | PROTEIN: 44g

Roasted Cornish Hen

Air fryer Cornish hens are delicious, juicy little roasted chickens that are done in less than 30 minutes of cooking time! These taste like a rotisserie chicken but are fresh and hot with an easy spice rub as the coating. They're great for a weeknight dinner but also a little fancy if you've got a special occasion dinner.

Hands-On Time: 5 minutes
Cook Time: 25 minutes

Serves 1

- 1 teaspoon coarse sea salt
- 1 teaspoon paprika
- ⅛ teaspoon red pepper flakes
- ½ teaspoon cayenne pepper
- 1 teaspoon onion powder
- ½ teaspoon ground white pepper
- ½ teaspoon garlic powder
- 1 teaspoon dried rosemary, crushed
- 1 Cornish hen
- ¼ white onion, roughly chopped
- ½ medium lemon, cut into wedges

1 In a small bowl, mix all spices. Rub spice mixture onto hen. Stuff hen with onion and lemon.

2 Place hen in air fryer and air fry at 400°F for 15 minutes. Open air fryer and flip hen. Air fry 10 minutes more.

3 Remove from air fryer and serve.

PER SERVING

CALORIES: 714 | FAT: 43g | SODIUM: 2,088mg | CARBOHYDRATES: 12g | FIBER: 3g | SUGAR: 3g | PROTEIN: 59g

Italian Turkey Meatballs

Ground turkey is a very lean protein, and the additions of onion, garlic, and Parmesan cheese come together to create a perfect meatball. These are also versatile—you can dip them in barbecue sauce or add them to spaghetti!

Hands-On Time: 10 minutes
Cook Time: 9 minutes

Serves 1

¼ pound ground turkey
1 large egg white
2 tablespoons bread crumbs
½ teaspoon dried minced onion
½ teaspoon minced garlic
2 tablespoons grated Parmesan cheese
1 teaspoon Italian seasoning
¼ teaspoon coarse sea salt

1 In a medium bowl, mix all ingredients. Gently shape mixture into 6 (1½") balls.

2 Spray air fryer basket with nonstick cooking spray. Place meatballs in air fryer basket in a single layer. Air fry at 360°F for 5 minutes. Open air fryer and turn meatballs. Air fry 4 minutes more.

3 Remove from air fryer and serve.

PER SERVING

CALORIES: 309 | FAT: 12g | SODIUM: 893mg | CARBOHYDRATES: 12g | FIBER: 1g | SUGAR: 1g | PROTEIN: 33g

Chicken Ranch Club Flatbread

This Chicken Ranch Club Flatbread is absolutely delicious! Because it doesn't come as a frozen meal, your air fryer will be saving you the potential health issues associated with preservatives!

Hands-On Time: 5 minutes
Cook Time: 3 minutes

Serves 1

1 (2-ounce) flatbread
½ cup precooked chicken breast strips
1 slice precooked bacon, diced
1 small Roma tomato, sliced
2 tablespoons shredded low-fat mozzarella cheese
1 tablespoon fat-free ranch dressing

1 Lay flatbread in air fryer basket. Top half of flatbread with chicken, bacon, tomato, mozzarella, and ranch dressing.

2 Fold flatbread over and lay a butter knife on top to hold top down. Air fry at 350°F for 3 minutes.

3 Remove from air fryer and serve.

PER SERVING

CALORIES: 384 | FAT: 12g | SODIUM: 1,135mg | CARBOHYDRATES: 38g | FIBER: 2g | SUGAR: 5g | PROTEIN: 29g

Apple and Sage Turkey Breast

Whether you're wanting to make yourself a mini Thanksgiving dinner or you're looking for a new way to enjoy turkey, this recipe will be a favorite! This turkey is coated in a delicious autumnal rub of rosemary, sage, and thyme and then topped with butter and apple slices. While this is cooking, the aroma will have you thinking Thanksgiving is about to explode right out of the air fryer!

Hands-On Time: 5 minutes
Cook Time: 20 minutes

Serves 1

½ teaspoon coarse sea salt
½ teaspoon ground sage
¼ teaspoon ground thyme
¼ teaspoon dried rosemary, crushed
½ teaspoon onion powder
¼ teaspoon ground black pepper
1 (8-ounce) turkey breast
2 tablespoons salted butter, cut into chunks
½ small apple, sliced

TURKEY BREAST

Not hungry enough for a full turkey breast? You can find turkey tenderloins, which are breast portions, in the meat section of your grocery store. Buy a package containing two or three breasts and freeze the portions individually.

1 Spray a small casserole dish with nonstick cooking spray.

2 In a small bowl, mix all spices. Rub spice mixture onto turkey and place turkey in prepared dish. Scatter butter over turkey. Place apple on and around turkey.

3 Place dish in air fryer. If your air fryer tray has a handle that doesn't allow you to set dish in flat, remove tray and set dish in bottom of air fryer basket. Air fry at 325°F for 20 minutes.

4 Using an instant-read thermometer, check to be sure internal temperature in thickest part of turkey is 155°F–160°F. If not hot enough, air fry 2–3 minutes more. Turkey temperature will continue to rise as turkey rests for 5–10 minutes and will reach 165°F.

5 Remove from the air fryer and serve.

PER SERVING

CALORIES: 461 | FAT: 25g | SODIUM: 1,557mg | CARBOHYDRATES: 10g | FIBER: 2g | SUGAR: 7g | PROTEIN: 48g

Orange Chicken

In this homage to a classic Chinese takeout dish, breaded chicken breast is air fried and then tossed in a light orange sauce. Air frying again after coating seals the sauce onto the chicken.

Hands-On Time: 10 minutes
Cook Time: 17 minutes

Serves 1

- 1 (4-ounce) chicken breast, cut into 1" cubes
- 1 large egg, beaten
- ¼ cup all-purpose flour
- 2 tablespoons cornstarch
- ⅟₁₆ teaspoon salt
- ⅟₁₆ teaspoon ground black pepper
- 1 large orange
- 1 teaspoon olive oil
- ½ teaspoon minced garlic
- 1 tablespoon hoisin sauce
- 2 tablespoons Korean barbecue sauce
- 2 teaspoons honey
- ⅟₁₆ teaspoon red pepper flakes
- ¾ cup cooked brown rice
- 1 teaspoon chopped fresh cilantro
- 1 teaspoon diced green onion

HOW TO ZEST FRUIT

All you need to zest fruit is a Microplane grater or a cheese grater. Run fruit over the smallest holes of the grater, going in one direction, and remove only the brightly colored rind. When you get to the white pith, move to another spot on the fruit.

1. Dip chicken pieces in egg and coat thoroughly. On a medium plate, mix flour, cornstarch, salt, and black pepper. Remove chicken pieces from egg and coat in flour mixture. Shake off excess flour and place chicken pieces in air fryer basket in a single layer. Spritz generously with olive oil spray until all flour is covered. Air fry at 375°F for 4 minutes. Open air fryer and flip chicken pieces. Spritz second side with olive oil spray. Air fry 4 minutes more.

2. Using a Microplane grater, zest orange and set zest aside. Slice orange in half and squeeze juice into a measuring cup, yielding ¼ cup juice.

3. While chicken is air frying, heat a medium skillet over medium-high heat. Add oil and garlic and sauté for 1 minute.

4. Add orange zest, orange juice, hoisin sauce, barbecue sauce, honey, and red pepper flakes to skillet and bring to a boil. Boil 3 minutes, stirring constantly. Reduce heat and simmer 1–2 minutes until sauce thickens, stirring frequently. Remove skillet from heat.

5. Remove chicken from air fryer and add to skillet. Coat each piece with sauce. Using tongs, return chicken to air fryer in a single layer. Air fry at 400°F for 4 minutes.

6. Place rice in a medium bowl. Remove chicken from air fryer and place on top of rice. Drizzle with excess sauce and top with cilantro and green onion. Serve.

PER SERVING

CALORIES: 604 | **FAT:** 11g | **SODIUM:** 1,089mg | **CARBOHYDRATES:** 92g | **FIBER:** 4g | **SUGAR:** 33g | **PROTEIN:** 34g

Parmesan-Crusted Chicken

Making Parmesan-Crusted Chicken in the air fryer takes only 15 minutes! Ordinary chicken becomes irresistible when it's topped with a creamy, crunchy Parmesan crust made of Caesar salad dressing, bread crumbs, garlic, and cheese.

Hands-On Time: 2 minutes
Cook Time: 13 minutes

Serves 1

- 1 (4-ounce) boneless, skinless chicken breast
- 2 tablespoons Caesar salad dressing
- ¼ cup grated Parmesan cheese, divided
- ¼ cup bread crumbs
- 1 teaspoon minced garlic
- 1 tablespoon salted butter, melted
- ¼ cup shredded Monterey jack cheese

1 Place chicken in air fryer and air fry at 350°F for 10 minutes.

2 While chicken is cooking, prepare toppings. In a small bowl, mix dressing and 2 tablespoons Parmesan. In a medium bowl, mix bread crumbs, garlic, remaining 2 tablespoons Parmesan, and butter.

3 Open air fryer and top chicken with Caesar mixture, then crumb mixture and Monterey jack. Air fry at 375°F for 3 minutes until cheese melts and toppings begin to brown.

4 Using a spatula, remove chicken from air fryer and serve.

PER SERVING

CALORIES: 653 | FAT: 39g | SODIUM: 1,141mg | CARBOHYDRATES: 25g | FIBER: 1g | SUGAR: 2g | PROTEIN: 44g

Santa Fe Chicken Wrap

This Santa Fe Chicken Wrap is a delicious lunchtime treat! It's also a favorite go-to for a healthy lunch. This wrap is filled with chicken, pepper jack cheese, ranch, and flavorful vegetables. Serve this tasty wrap with some salsa to dip it in.

Hands-On Time: 5 minutes
Cook Time: 5 minutes

Serves 1

- ½ (4-ounce) boneless, skinless chicken breast, cooked, cut into strips
- 1 (6") low-carb tortilla
- 1 (1-ounce) slice pepper jack cheese, cut into strips
- 1 small Roma tomato, sliced
- 1 (1"-thick) slice red onion, halved, rings separated
- 1 tablespoon ranch dressing
- 1 tablespoon salsa
- 1 teaspoon buffalo sauce

1. If chicken is cold, place on microwave-safe plate and microwave 30 seconds.

2. On tortilla, lay out pepper jack, chicken, tomato, and onion. Drizzle ranch dressing, salsa, and buffalo sauce over top of chicken. Tightly roll tortilla, leaving ends open.

3. Lay wrap seam-side down in air fryer basket and spritz with olive oil spray. Air fry at 400°F for 2 minutes.

4. Open air fryer, flip wrap, and spritz again with olive oil spray. Air fry 2 minutes more.

5. Using tongs, carefully remove wrap from air fryer and serve.

PER SERVING

CALORIES: 436 | **FAT:** 19g | **SODIUM:** 874mg | **CARBOHYDRATES:** 34g | **FIBER:** 13g | **SUGAR:** 10g | **PROTEIN:** 39g

Chicken Popper Wrap

This Chicken Popper Wrap is a copycat wrap from a fast-food restaurant chain! It's so delicious that it's hard to believe it's healthy. This wrap is filled with chicken, cream cheese, jalapeños, and yummy vegetables. You'll want to make it every day!

Hands-On Time: 5 minutes
Cook Time: 5 minutes

Serves 1

- ½ (4-ounce) boneless, skinless chicken breast, cooked, cut into strips
- 3 tablespoons low-fat cream cheese
- 1 (6") low-carb tortilla
- 2 tablespoons low-fat ranch dressing
- 1 small Roma tomato, sliced
- 1 (1"-thick) slice red onion, halved, rings separated
- 2 tablespoons pickled jalapeño rings
- 2 tablespoons salsa

1   If chicken is cold, place on microwave-safe plate and microwave 30 seconds.

2   Spread cream cheese on half of tortilla. Top cream cheese with ranch dressing, chicken, tomato, onion, and jalapeños. Tightly roll tortilla, leaving ends open.

3   Lay wrap seam-side down in air fryer basket and spritz with olive oil spray. Air fry at 400°F for 2 minutes.

4   Open air fryer, flip wrap, and spritz again with olive oil spray. Air fry 2 minutes more.

5   Using tongs, carefully remove wrap from air fryer. Serve with salsa for dipping.

PER SERVING

CALORIES: 376 | **FAT:** 15g | **SODIUM:** 1,243mg | **CARBOHYDRATES:** 41g | **FIBER:** 14g | **SUGAR:** 12g | **PROTEIN:** 23g

Marinated Chicken Breast

This simple Marinated Chicken Breast is perfect to use in wraps or serve over pasta or salads. It's also great with side dishes like Potato Pancakes or Roasted Asparagus, both in Chapter 4.

Hands-On Time: 3 minutes

Cook Time: 12 minutes

Serves 1

¼ cup Italian dressing

1 (4-ounce) boneless, skinless chicken breast

1 Pour dressing into a quart-sized plastic zip-top bag and add chicken. Marinate in refrigerator at least 1 hour, up to overnight.

2 Remove chicken from zip-top bag and discard marinade. Open air fryer and place chicken in air fryer basket. Air fry at 350°F for 6 minutes.

3 Open air fryer and flip chicken. Air fry 6 minutes more.

4 Using tongs, carefully remove chicken from air fryer. Slice and serve.

PER SERVING

CALORIES: 137 | **FAT:** 4g | **SODIUM:** 100mg | **CARBOHYDRATES:** 1g | **FIBER:** 0g | **SUGAR:** 1g | **PROTEIN:** 25g

Chicken Cordon Bleu

Chicken Cordon Bleu sounds fancy but is easy and fast to make, especially in an air fryer. Chicken breast rolled with ham and Swiss cheese is breaded and then air fried. This dish pairs well with the Crispy Brussels Sprouts and No-Yeast Dinner Biscuits in Chapter 4. Add on the decadent Chocolate Melting Cake from Chapter 9 for dessert!

Hands-On Time: 10 minutes
Cook Time: 14 minutes

Serves 1

- 2 (4-ounce) boneless, skinless chicken tenders
- 1 tablespoon Dijon mustard
- 2 (1-ounce) thin slices deli ham
- 2 (1-ounce) thin slices Swiss cheese
- 1 large egg, beaten
- ½ cup panko bread crumbs
- 2 tablespoons grated Parmesan cheese

1 Place chicken on parchment paper and fold parchment over top of chicken. Using a meat tenderizer, lightly pound chicken to an even thickness.

2 Spread mustard on top of chicken. Lay 1 slice ham and 1 slice cheese on top of mustard on each chicken tender. Tightly roll up each chicken tender so ham and cheese are on the inside of the roll.

3 Prepare breading station with two medium dishes. Place egg in the first dish. Mix panko and Parmesan with a fork in the second dish. Dip each chicken roll in egg, then dredge each roll in panko mixture, coating all sides.

4 Place chicken rolls in air fryer basket. Spritz with olive oil spray. Air fry at 350°F for 14 minutes.

5 Using an instant-read thermometer, check to be sure internal temperature of chicken rolls is 160°F–165°F. Using silicone tongs, carefully remove chicken rolls from air fryer and serve.

PER SERVING

CALORIES: 741 | **FAT:** 30g | **SODIUM:** 1,326mg | **CARBOHYDRATES:** 27g | **FIBER:** 1g | **SUGAR:** 2g | **PROTEIN:** 84g

Chicken Parmesan

Air fryer Chicken Parmesan may astound you with how easy and filling it is! This chicken is coated with bread crumbs and cheese, and it is perfect served over pasta. In less than 30 minutes, you'll have a delicious dinner with a homemade Alfredo sauce to go with it!

Hands-On Time: 10 minutes
Cook Time: 15 minutes

Serves 1

Chicken Parmesan
¼ cup all-purpose flour
1 large egg, beaten
½ cup Italian bread crumbs
2 tablespoons grated
    Parmesan cheese
½ teaspoon salt
1 (4-ounce) boneless,
    skinless chicken breast
¼ cup jarred marinara sauce
1 (1-ounce) slice fresh
    mozzarella cheese
1 cup cooked spaghetti

Alfredo Sauce
3 tablespoons salted butter
1 teaspoon minced garlic
1 teaspoon all-purpose flour
⅓ cup half-and-half
2 tablespoons grated
    Parmesan cheese

1. To make Chicken Parmesan: Prepare breading station with three medium dishes. Spread flour in the first dish. Place egg in the second dish. Mix bread crumbs, Parmesan, and salt with a fork in the third dish.

2. Place chicken on parchment paper and fold parchment over top of chicken. Using a meat tenderizer, lightly pound chicken to an even thickness. Coat chicken in flour, then dip in egg, and then coat in bread crumb mixture. Place chicken in air fryer basket. Spritz with olive oil spray. Air fry at 350°F for 8 minutes.

3. Open air fryer, flip chicken, and spritz again with olive oil spray. Spread marinara on top of chicken. Top with mozzarella. Close air fryer and air fry 6 minutes more.

4. To make Alfredo Sauce: Melt butter in a small skillet over medium-high heat. Add garlic and cook 30 seconds. Add flour and whisk until incorporated. Add half-and-half and Parmesan and whisk until sauce begins to simmer. Remove skillet from heat.

5. Place cooked pasta in a medium bowl. Top with Alfredo Sauce. Remove chicken from air fryer and place on top of Alfredo. Serve.

PER SERVING

CALORIES: 1,126 | FAT: 57g | SODIUM: 2,542mg | CARBOHYDRATES: 90g | FIBER: 6g | SUGAR: 9g | PROTEIN: 54g

Sweet and Spicy Chicken Legs

If you're in the mood for something sweet and hot, try these tender and juicy chicken legs! This chicken dish has a simple marinade with items you likely already have in your pantry. You could also use bone-in chicken thighs for this recipe.

Hands-On Time: 5 minutes
Cook Time: 20 minutes

Serves 1

1 tablespoon light brown sugar
½ teaspoon red pepper flakes
½ teaspoon ground cumin
1 teaspoon smoked paprika
1 teaspoon garlic powder
1 teaspoon lemon juice
1 tablespoon olive oil
2 (4-ounce) chicken legs

1 In a gallon-sized plastic zip-top bag, mix all ingredients except chicken. Be sure all ingredients are well incorporated. Add chicken and marinate in refrigerator at least 30 minutes, up to overnight.

2 Remove chicken from bag and place in air fryer basket. Air fry at 400°F for 10 minutes.

3 Open air fryer and flip chicken, then air fry 10 minutes more.

4 Using an instant-read thermometer, check to be sure internal temperature in thickest part of chicken is 160°F–165°F. Using silicone tongs, carefully remove chicken and serve.

PER SERVING

CALORIES: 511 | FAT: 27g | SODIUM: 176mg | CARBOHYDRATES: 18g | FIBER: 2g | SUGAR: 14g | PROTEIN: 43g

Garlic Parmesan Chicken Wings

Chicken wings are fantastic and easy in the air fryer! You can even cheat and throw in frozen, pre-seasoned ones! These from-scratch Garlic Parmesan Chicken Wings will make you think you're at the sports bar without ever leaving your kitchen.

Hands-On Time: 3 minutes
Cook Time: 21 minutes

Serves 1

2 tablespoons salted butter
¼ cup grated Parmesan cheese
½ teaspoon salt
Juice of ½ medium lemon
½ teaspoon plus ¹⁄₁₆ teaspoon garlic salt, divided
6 (3-ounce) chicken wings

1 In a medium microwave-safe bowl, combine butter, Parmesan, salt, lemon juice, and ½ teaspoon garlic salt. Cover and microwave 45 seconds to melt, then stir to combine. Place wings in another medium bowl and toss them in butter sauce.

2 Place wings in air fryer basket. Sprinkle with remaining ¹⁄₁₆ teaspoon garlic salt. Air fry at 350°F for 10 minutes.

3 Open air fryer and flip wings. Increase temperature to 400°F and air fry 10 minutes more.

4 Using silicone tongs, carefully remove wings and serve.

PER SERVING

CALORIES: 1,604 | FAT: 110g | SODIUM: 3,396mg | CARBOHYDRATES: 4g | FIBER: 0g | SUGAR: 0g | PROTEIN: 129g

Chicken Teriyaki Sandwich

You can find a chicken teriyaki sandwich at nearly every sub shop. This recipe will show you how to make an even better one in the comfort of your home! It's loaded with green pepper, mushrooms, onion, and cheese to make a delicious, hearty sandwich in minutes.

Hands-On Time: 5 minutes
Cook Time: 10 minutes

Serves 1

1 (4-ounce) boneless, skinless chicken breast, sliced into strips
¼ medium green bell pepper, sliced
4 button mushrooms, sliced
2 (1"-thick) slices white onion, halved, rings separated
¼ cup teriyaki sauce
2 (1-ounce) slices Swiss cheese
1 sub roll

1 Place chicken and vegetables in a medium bowl and toss them in teriyaki sauce. Place chicken and vegetables in air fryer basket. Air fry at 350°F for 5 minutes.

2 Open air fryer. Using silicone tongs, toss chicken and vegetables. Air fry 3 minutes more.

3 Open air fryer and push chicken and vegetables to one side of air fryer basket. Place cheese slices on top of chicken and vegetables. Open sub roll and place open-side down on other side of air fryer basket. Air fry at 300°F for 2 minutes.

4 Remove sub roll and set on a medium plate. Using a thin metal spatula, remove cheese-topped chicken and vegetables and place on toasted sub roll. Serve.

PER SERVING

CALORIES: 767 | FAT: 24g | SODIUM: 3,107mg | CARBOHYDRATES: 86g | FIBER: 10g | SUGAR: 31g | PROTEIN: 59g

Caprese-Stuffed Chicken Breasts

Caprese salad is a delicious spring salad with fresh basil and tomato, alongside fresh mozzarella cheese and a tart balsamic glaze. This recipe takes every delicious bite of that springtime favorite and adds it to air fryer roasted chicken. You will want to use a large, thick chicken breast for this recipe.

Hands-On Time: 10 minutes
Cook Time: 12 minutes

Serves 1

- 1 (6-ounce) boneless, skinless chicken breast
- 2 (1-ounce) slices fresh mozzarella, halved
- 1 medium Roma tomato, halved lengthwise, then thinly sliced
- 4 fresh spinach leaves
- 4 fresh basil leaves
- ½ teaspoon olive oil
- 1 tablespoon balsamic glaze
- ⅟₁₆ teaspoon coarse sea salt
- ⅟₁₆ teaspoon ground black pepper
- ½ teaspoon Italian seasoning

1 Place chicken breast on a cutting board and cut five or six slits in it, being careful not to cut through completely.

2 Place chicken in air fryer. Stuff mozzarella, tomato, spinach, and basil into slits in chicken.

3 In a small bowl, whisk oil, balsamic glaze, salt, pepper, and Italian seasoning. Baste chicken with mixture.

4 Air fry at 370°F for 12 minutes. Using an instant-read thermometer, check to be sure internal temperature in thickest part of chicken is 160°F–165°F. If not hot enough, air fry 2 minutes more until chicken reaches safe temperature.

5 Remove chicken from air fryer and serve.

PER SERVING

CALORIES: 386 | FAT: 14g | SODIUM: 292mg | CARBOHYDRATES: 19g | FIBER: 1g | SUGAR: 18g | PROTEIN: 46g

Crunchy Buffalo Chicken Bites

These spicy Crunchy Buffalo Chicken Bites are perfect as an appetizer or a main dish. Plus, you can make them as spicy or mild as you like, depending on the sauce you use. You can also leave the breading off if you want to have "naked" chicken bites. These will be spicy, so be sure to have some ranch dressing on the side!

Hands-On Time: 15 minutes
Cook Time: 7 minutes

Serves 1

1 (4-ounce) boneless, skinless chicken breast
¼ cup buffalo sauce
1 cup panko bread crumbs

SPICY PANKO BREAD CRUMBS

If you want to make this dish a little spicier, you may be able to find a spicy blend of panko bread crumbs in the grocery store. If you can't find those, you can add 1 teaspoon of chili powder, cayenne pepper, or chipotle seasoning to your panko bread crumbs for a DIY spicy panko mixture.

1 Cut chicken into 1" pieces.

2 Prepare breading station with two medium dishes. Place buffalo sauce in the first dish and spread panko in the second dish. Toss chicken in buffalo sauce, then dredge in panko, coating all sides.

3 Place chicken in air fryer basket and spritz with olive oil spray. Air fry at 350°F for 3 minutes.

4 Open air fryer. Using silicone tongs, flip chicken. Spritz again with olive oil spray. Air fry 4 minutes more.

5 Remove chicken from air fryer and serve.

PER SERVING

CALORIES: 319 | FAT: 4g | SODIUM: 1,071mg | CARBOHYDRATES: 40g | FIBER: 0g | SUGAR: 2g | PROTEIN: 30g

Greek Chicken Kebabs

Looking to change up your dinner? Try these air fryer chicken kebabs. The variety of textures will keep your mouth happy. This recipe adds a lemony twist with Greek seasoning and a delicious basting sauce that doubles as a dipping sauce! Plus, when you cut everything into bite-sized pieces, it all cooks so fast. A squeeze of lemon juice gives the finished kebabs a brighter flavor.

Hands-On Time: 10 minutes
Cook Time: 10 minutes

Serves 1

1 (4-ounce) boneless, skinless chicken breast
2 mini sweet peppers
½ small red onion, peeled
6 button mushrooms
6 cherry tomatoes
⅓ cup nonfat plain Greek yogurt
1 teaspoon Greek seasoning
1 teaspoon olive oil
1 tablespoon lemon juice

1 Cut chicken into 1½" pieces. Cut peppers, onion, and mushrooms into pieces of approximately the same size as chicken.

2 On six short wooden skewers, alternate pieces of chicken, peppers, onion, and mushrooms, along with tomatoes.

3 In a medium bowl, mix yogurt, Greek seasoning, oil, and lemon juice. Using a silicone baster, baste sauce onto all sides of chicken and vegetables. Place skewers in air fryer basket. Air fry at 360°F for 5 minutes.

4 Open air fryer. Using silicone tongs, flip skewers. Air fry 5 minutes more.

5 Remove skewers from air fryer and serve with remaining sauce.

PER SERVING

CALORIES: 309 | **FAT:** 11g | **SODIUM:** 1,043mg | **CARBOHYDRATES:** 18g | **FIBER:** 4g | **SUGAR:** 12g | **PROTEIN:** 37g

Spicy Soy-Glazed Chicken Thighs

Bone-in chicken thighs are an incredibly affordable cut of meat. They also pack the most flavor of any chicken you'll try. This Asian glaze is delicious, with a sweet and spicy flavor profile. Serve with rice.

Hands-On Time: 5 minutes
Cook Time: 25 minutes

Serves 1

2 tablespoons soy sauce
1 tablespoon balsamic
    vinegar
1 teaspoon honey
½ teaspoon minced garlic
¼ teaspoon sriracha
¼ teaspoon minced fresh
    ginger
2 (4½-ounce) bone-in, skin-
    on chicken thighs

1 In a gallon-sized plastic zip-top bag, combine soy sauce, vinegar, honey, garlic, sriracha, and ginger. Seal bag and mix contents. Add chicken to bag and seal. Marinate in refrigerator at least 30 minutes, up to overnight.

2 Remove chicken from refrigerator, discard marinade, and place chicken skin-side down in air fryer. Air fry at 400°F for 15 minutes.

3 Open air fryer and flip chicken. Lower temperature to 370°F and air fry 10 minutes more.

4 Using an instant-read thermometer, check to be sure internal temperature in thickest part of chicken is 160°F–165°F. If not hot enough, air fry 2–3 minutes more. Remove chicken from air fryer and serve.

PER SERVING

CALORIES: 594 | **FAT:** 35g | **SODIUM:** 373mg | **CARBOHYDRATES:** 1g | **FIBER:** 0g | **SUGAR:** 1g | **PROTEIN:** 59g

Cheesy Chicken Tostada

This air fryer Cheesy Chicken Tostada will give you all the fast food feels without a trip to the drive-through. Start with a tortilla and top it with fajita chicken, refried beans, lots of cheese, sour cream, and salsa for a delicious, crunchy dinner in minutes.

Hands-On Time: 5 minutes
Cook Time: 13 minutes

Serves 1

- ½ (4-ounce) boneless, skinless chicken breast, thinly sliced
- 1 mini sweet pepper, thinly sliced
- 1 (1"-thick) slice yellow onion, diced
- 1 tablespoon Tajín Clásico Seasoning
- 1 teaspoon olive oil
- 1 (6") low-carb flour tortilla
- 1⁄16 teaspoon coarse sea salt
- ¼ cup refried beans
- ¼ cup shredded Colby jack cheese
- 2 tablespoons salsa
- 2 tablespoons sour cream

SUBSTITUTE PRECOOKED CHICKEN

If you have precooked chicken, you can easily use that in this recipe. Mix with Tajín seasoning and vegetables and air fry 4 minutes to reheat, instead of 7 minutes. Then proceed with the remainder of the recipe.

1 In a medium bowl, combine chicken, pepper, onion, Tajín seasoning, and oil. Toss to coat.

2 Place chicken and vegetables in air fryer basket. Air fry at 360°F for 7 minutes, then remove chicken and vegetables from air fryer basket.

3 Lay tortilla in air fryer and spritz with olive oil spray. Keep tortilla flat by laying two butter knives across it. This also prevents tortilla from blowing around in air fryer. Air fry at 360°F for 2 minutes.

4 Open air fryer. Using tongs, remove butter knives and flip tortilla. Spritz with olive oil spray, sprinkle with salt, and replace butter knives. Air fry 2 minutes more.

5 Open air fryer and transfer tortilla to cutting board. Top tortilla with beans, chicken, vegetables, and Colby jack. Using a spatula, return tostada to air fryer. Air fry at 350°F for 2 minutes.

6 Remove from air fryer and serve with salsa and sour cream.

PER SERVING

CALORIES: 453 | **FAT:** 21g | **SODIUM:** 3,348mg | **CARBOHYDRATES:** 42g | **FIBER:** 16g | **SUGAR:** 11g | **PROTEIN:** 30g

Buffalo Cheddar Crispy Chicken

Cheesy, crispy, buttery, crunchy, spicy, and juicy—all words to describe the perfect chicken dinner. Topping chicken with a mixture of mayonnaise and buffalo sauce and then adding a pretzel crust results in a fantastic chicken dinner. This will change the way you think about chicken breasts.

Hands-On Time: 5 minutes
Cook Time: 11 minutes

Serves 1

- 1 teaspoon mayonnaise
- 1 teaspoon buffalo sauce
- 1 (4-ounce) boneless, skinless chicken breast
- 2 tablespoons hot buffalo wing pretzels, crumbled
- 2 tablespoons shredded Cheddar cheese
- 1 tablespoon salted butter, melted

HOW TO BUY CHICKEN BREASTS

Though convenience is important when cooking for one, so is price. Large value packs of chicken are the more affordable option in the long run, but for convenience, you can pick up some frozen prepackaged chicken breasts. Pay attention to chicken breast size, as small ones cook in 10 minutes, while larger ones take 13–15 minutes.

1 In a small bowl, mix mayonnaise and buffalo sauce.

2 Place chicken in air fryer and pour mayonnaise mixture on top. Air fry at 350°F for 8 minutes.

3 In a small bowl, combine pretzels, Cheddar, and butter.

4 When chicken is done, open air fryer and top chicken with pretzel mixture. Press mixture onto chicken. Air fry 3–5 minutes more. Using an instant-read thermometer, check to be sure internal temperature in thickest part of chicken is 160°F–165°F. If not hot enough, air fry 1–2 minutes more. Using a spatula, remove chicken from air fryer and serve.

PER SERVING

CALORIES: 313 | FAT: 17g | SODIUM: 529mg | CARBOHYDRATES: 12g | FIBER: 0g | SUGAR: 1g | PROTEIN: 26g

Breaded Chicken Breast

Chicken breast is such an easy go-to for dinner, but it's nice to have a variety of ways to prepare it. Adding mayonnaise keeps the chicken juicy, and the panko adds a delicious crunch! This chicken is also delicious sliced on top of your favorite salad or with a side of vegetables.

Hands-On Time: 5 minutes
Cook Time: 14 minutes

Serves 1

1 (4-ounce) boneless,
   skinless chicken breast
2 tablespoons mayonnaise
¼ cup panko bread crumbs
¹⁄₁₆ teaspoon coarse sea salt

1　Brush chicken with mayonnaise on both sides.

2　On a medium plate, stir together panko and salt. Dredge chicken in panko mixture, coating both sides.

3　Open air fryer and place chicken in air fryer basket. Spritz with olive oil spray. Air fry at 350°F for 7 minutes.

4　Open air fryer, flip chicken, and spritz again with olive oil spray. Air fry 7 minutes more.

5　Using tongs, remove chicken from air fryer. Slice and serve.

PER SERVING

CALORIES: 410 | FAT: 24g | SODIUM: 392mg | CARBOHYDRATES: 20g | FIBER: 0g | SUGAR: 1g | PROTEIN: 28g

6

Beef and Pork

Though not as affordable as turkey or chicken, beef and pork can still be budget-friendly choices for dinner. They each come in a variety of cuts, so whether you're looking for something lean and healthy or something fatty and flavorful, there are plenty of options. Whether you're using ground beef or pork, steaks, chops, or any other cut, you can always use some fun new options for dinner. Plus, you can bet that these will be simple and fast recipes, as they are for your air fryer!

This chapter covers unique and new ideas for beef and pork, as well as basic techniques that are great any night of the week. This chapter will give you the key to cooking delicious basics such as The Perfect Rib Eye, Crispy Pork Belly, and Mom's Meatloaf. However, if you're looking for a unique dish to add to your menu, try the Taco-Stuffed Avocado, Pepperoni Pizzadilla, or Cheeseburger Onion Rings. Get cooking!

The Perfect Rib Eye

You can make the perfect steak in your air fryer. No need for a grill, a cast iron skillet, or a mess! Start with a quality steak, at least 1" thick, with nice marbling. Then, add seasoning. This can be as simple as salt and pepper, or you can use a premade steak seasoning. Try Worcestershire sauce on your finished air fryer rib eye—it's delicious!

Hands-On Time: 5 minutes
Cook Time: 9 minutes

Serves 1

- 1 (8-ounce) boneless rib eye steak
- 2 tablespoons steak seasoning

STEAK OPTIONS

You can cook any cut of steak you like in the air fryer. Keep thickness in mind when setting the cooking time. Larger, thicker cuts of steak will take longer than a thin-cut steak. New York strip and sirloin are comparable to rib eye in terms of seasoning and cooking times.

1 Coat all sides of steak with steak seasoning. Set steak on a wire rack over a large plate and refrigerate at least 1 hour, up to overnight. Remove steak from refrigerator and allow to come to room temperature 30–60 minutes before cooking.

2 Place steak in air fryer basket and air fry at 375°F for 5 minutes.

3 Open air fryer and flip steak. Air fry 4 minutes more for medium-rare, 6 minutes for medium, or 8 minutes for well done. Using an instant-read thermometer, check internal temperature: 135°F for medium-rare, 145°F for medium, 155°F for medium well, or 165°F for well done.

4 Remove steak from air fryer and place on a cutting board. Tent with aluminum foil and let rest 5–10 minutes. Slice steak against the grain and serve.

PER SERVING

CALORIES: 372 | FAT: 14g | SODIUM: 4,184mg | CARBOHYDRATES: 0g | FIBER: 0g | SUGAR: 0g | PROTEIN: 54g

Crispy Pork Belly

Pork belly is a delightfully indulgent treat! It's basically a thick slab of uncut, uncured bacon. So, if you like bacon, you'll like pork belly—especially in your air fryer. Topping it with barbecue sauce and seasoning creates a smoky, savory flavor.

Hands-On Time: 5 minutes
Cook Time: 23 minutes

Serves 1

½ pound pork belly
2 tablespoons barbecue seasoning for pork
2 tablespoons barbecue sauce

1   Slice pork belly with a boning knife. If pork belly is thick, cut into slabs ¾" thick. If pork belly is thin, cut into 1" cubes.

2   Coat all sides of pork belly with barbecue seasoning and place in air fryer. Be sure to leave space between pieces. Air fry at 200°F for 10 minutes.

3   Open air fryer basket and, using tongs, flip pork belly. Air fry 10 minutes more.

4   Open air fryer and drizzle pork belly with barbecue sauce. Close air fryer and air fry at 370°F for 3 minutes.

5   Remove pork belly from air fryer and serve.

PER SERVING

CALORIES: 618 | **FAT:** 50g | **SODIUM:** 2,541mg | **CARBOHYDRATES:** 15g | **FIBER:** 0g | **SUGAR:** 11g | **PROTEIN:** 23g

Barbecued Country-Style Ribs

Country-style ribs are one of the most affordable cuts of pork and one of the easiest to cook. This recipe is super simple, with just a spice rub and an air fryer. Country-style ribs aren't really ribs in the traditional sense. If you like them saucy, add your favorite barbecue sauce and air fry an additional 3–4 minutes to bake it on.

Hands-On Time: 5 minutes
Cook Time: 18 minutes

Serves 1

- 1 tablespoon light brown sugar
- 1 teaspoon paprika
- 1 teaspoon ground black pepper
- 1 teaspoon coarse sea salt
- 1 teaspoon garlic powder
- 1 teaspoon onion powder
- ½ teaspoon dry mustard
- ½ pound country-style pork ribs

WHAT ARE COUNTRY-STYLE RIBS?

Country-style ribs aren't ribs at all. They are tender pieces cut from the pig's shoulder and are like blade steak. They have more meat and less bone than traditional ribs. The cut is very affordable, and you can often find them in a boneless cut.

1 Mix together all seasonings in a small bowl. Rub seasoning mix into all sides of ribs.

2 Place ribs in air fryer basket with 1" of space between them. Air fry at 370°F for 18 minutes.

3 Using an instant-read thermometer, check to be sure internal temperature of ribs is at least 145°F. If not hot enough, air fry 2–3 minutes more.

4 Remove from air fryer and serve!

PER SERVING

CALORIES: 458 | **FAT:** 19g | **SODIUM:** 2,048mg | **CARBOHYDRATES:** 21g | **FIBER:** 2g | **SUGAR:** 14g | **PROTEIN:** 51g

Ham Steak

This recipe uses pineapple in a fruit cup size, which is great when cooking for one. Make a side of Crispy Brussels Sprouts and No-Yeast Dinner Biscuits, both from Chapter 4.

Hands-On Time: 2 minutes
Cook Time: 10 minutes

Serves 1

1 (4-ounce) ham steak
1 tablespoon light brown sugar
1 (4-ounce) cup pineapple tidbits

1   Place ham steak in air fryer. Air fry at 370°F for 5 minutes.

2   Open air fryer and flip ham steak. Sprinkle with sugar and place pineapple on top of ham steak. Air fry 5 minutes more.

3   Remove ham steak from air fryer and serve.

PER SERVING

CALORIES: 307 | **FAT:** 8g | **SODIUM:** 1,574mg | **CARBOHYDRATES:** 32g | **FIBER:** 2g | **SUGAR:** 30g | **PROTEIN:** 26g

Sausage and Peppers

Air fryer Sausage and Peppers are a 10-minute weeknight meal. This recipe uses uncooked Italian sausage, but you can also use smoked sausage. If using smoked sausage, cut the cook time down to 6 minutes.

Hands-On Time: 5 minutes
Cook Time: 10 minutes

Serves 1

1 (4-ounce) Italian sausage link
2 mini sweet peppers, sliced
1 (1"-thick) slice sweet yellow onion, halved, rings separated
1 teaspoon olive oil
½ teaspoon seasoning salt

1   Place sausage, peppers, and onion in air fryer. Sprinkle with oil and seasoning salt. Air fry at 400°F for 10 minutes.

2   Remove from air fryer and serve.

PER SERVING

CALORIES: 407 | **FAT:** 27g | **SODIUM:** 1,792mg | **CARBOHYDRATES:** 21g | **FIBER:** 3g | **SUGAR:** 9g | **PROTEIN:** 19g

Steak Fajitas

Steak Fajitas are a go-to dinner that is on the table in about 15 minutes. Peppers, onion, steak, and fajita seasoning all come together deliciously. Bring out the toppings too: sour cream, cheese, salsa—and more if you're feeling adventurous! If you're not familiar with Tajín Clásico Seasoning, it's a must-have chili-lime seasoning that is perfect for fajitas.

Hands-On Time: 5 minutes
Cook Time: 11 minutes

Serves 1

- 1 (8-ounce) skirt steak, thinly sliced
- 2 mini sweet peppers, thinly sliced
- ⅓ cup chopped yellow onion
- 1 tablespoon Tajín Clásico Seasoning
- 1 teaspoon olive oil
- 2 (6") low-carb flour tortillas
- ¼ cup shredded Colby jack cheese
- 2 tablespoons salsa
- 2 tablespoons sour cream

STEAK OPTIONS

If skirt steak is too hard to find, you can replace it with flank steak, hanger, or sirloin. If you use a tougher cut of meat like eye of round or sirloin, you will want to marinate the meat overnight. A store-bought mojo criollo marinade is perfect for fajitas.

1 In a medium bowl, add steak, peppers, onion, Tajín seasoning, and oil. Toss to coat.

2 Place steak and vegetables in air fryer basket. Air fry at 375°F for 5 minutes.

3 Open air fryer and, using tongs, toss steak and vegetables. Air fry 5 minutes more, then remove steak and vegetables from air fryer basket.

4 Lay tortillas in air fryer. Keep tortillas flat by laying two butter knives across them. Air fry at 360°F for 1 minute to warm.

5 Open air fryer and transfer tortillas to a large plate. Top tortillas with steak, vegetables, Colby jack, salsa, and sour cream. Serve.

PER SERVING

CALORIES: 745 | FAT: 41g | SODIUM: 3,317mg | CARBOHYDRATES: 42g | FIBER: 21g | SUGAR: 8g | PROTEIN: 62g

Mom's Meatloaf

Your mother's meatloaf never tasted this good! This mini meatloaf will give you that homemade, savory taste with very little effort. This meatloaf uses ground pork instead of ground beef, as it makes the meatloaf more flavorful and likely cheaper too!

Hands-On Time: 10 minutes
Cook Time: 19 minutes

Serves 1

1 tablespoon diced yellow onion
1 mini sweet pepper, diced
1 baby carrot, grated
1 teaspoon olive oil
⅓ pound ground pork
½ teaspoon dried thyme
1 teaspoon Worcestershire sauce
1 teaspoon ketchup
1 tablespoon bread crumbs
1 teaspoon 2% milk
¹⁄₁₆ teaspoon coarse sea salt
¹⁄₁₆ teaspoon ground black pepper
2 tablespoons barbecue sauce

1 In a small bowl, combine onion, mini sweet pepper, carrot, and oil and toss to coat. Transfer to a small baking dish. Place dish in air fryer and air fry at 400°F for 4 minutes.

2 In a medium bowl, combine pork, thyme, Worcestershire sauce, ketchup, bread crumbs, milk, salt, and black pepper. Add vegetable mixture from air fryer and mix well.

3 Spray a mini loaf pan with nonstick cooking spray and place pork mixture in loaf pan. Spread barbecue sauce on top of meatloaf.

4 Place pan in air fryer and air fry at 370°F for 15 minutes. Using an instant-read thermometer, check to be sure internal temperature in center of loaf is 165°F. If not hot enough, air fry 2–3 minutes more.

5 Using pot holders, remove pan from air fryer, let meatloaf cool 5 minutes, and serve!

PER SERVING

CALORIES: 486 | FAT: 26g | SODIUM: 740mg | CARBOHYDRATES: 28g | FIBER: 2g | SUGAR: 16g | PROTEIN: 29g

Taco-Stuffed Avocado

This Taco-Stuffed Avocado is a great way to enjoy a low-carb taco with extra avocado! Fill an avocado with taco meat and your favorite toppings for a delicious, quick dinner. This recipe is great for leftover ground beef or pork.

Hands-On Time: 10 minutes
Cook Time: 10 minutes

Serves 1

¼ pound 80/20 ground beef
1 tablespoon taco seasoning
1 tablespoon water
1 small avocado, halved and pitted, peel intact
2 tablespoons shredded Colby jack cheese
2 cherry tomatoes, diced
1 tablespoon sour cream

1 In a small skillet, over medium-high heat, cook beef on stove top until cooked through and no pink is showing. Add taco seasoning and water. Stir until sauce forms, then remove from heat.

2 Scoop out some avocado flesh around the hole where the pit was to make a nice round space in each avocado. Set this avocado flesh aside in a small bowl.

3 Place avocado halves in air fryer basket. Spoon taco meat into each avocado half and top with Colby jack. Air fry at 350°F for 10 minutes.

4 Using tongs, carefully remove avocado halves from air fryer. Top with tomatoes, sour cream, and reserved avocado. Serve.

PER SERVING

CALORIES: 553 | FAT: 37g | SODIUM: 788mg | CARBOHYDRATES: 19g | FIBER: 11g | SUGAR: 3g | PROTEIN: 28g

Bacon Cheeseburger

Making a bacon cheeseburger just like you'd get at a restaurant is easy, and it's on the table in less than 15 minutes. Salt and pepper are the only seasonings you need for a delicious burger. Add all your favorite toppings!

Hands-On Time: 5 minutes
Cook Time: 9 minutes

Serves 1

⅓ pound 80/20 ground beef
1 strip bacon, cut in half
¼ teaspoon salt, divided
¼ teaspoon ground black
  pepper, divided
1 (1-ounce) slice American
  cheese
1 hamburger bun

1   Form beef into a round patty about 1" thick. Using your thumb, make a slight indentation in center of patty.

2   Place burger and bacon in air fryer basket. Sprinkle burger with ⅛ teaspoon each salt and pepper. Air fry at 375°F for 5 minutes.

3   Open air fryer and flip burger and bacon. Sprinkle burger with remaining ⅛ teaspoon each salt and pepper. Air fry 3 minutes more.

4   Open air fryer and remove bacon. Lay bacon on paper towel. Lay cheese on top of burger and secure it with a toothpick. Open hamburger bun and place open-side down in air fryer basket. Air fry 1–2 minutes more to melt cheese, warm bun, and get burger to desired temperature. Using an instant-read thermometer, check internal temperature: 135°F for medium-rare, 145°F for medium, 155°F for medium well, or 165°F for well done.

5   Once burger is at desired temperature, remove bun and burger. Serve cheeseburger on bun, topped with bacon and your favorite toppings.

PER SERVING

CALORIES: 510 | **FAT:** 23g | **SODIUM:** 1,428mg | **CARBOHYDRATES:** 25g | **FIBER:** 1g | **SUGAR:** 5g | **PROTEIN:** 41g

Garlic Butter Steak Bites with Mushrooms and Zucchini

These mouthwatering steak bites are complemented by delicious mushrooms and zucchini. Perfect for a low-carb diet, this steak will be perfectly browned on the outside and juicy on the inside. The cook time for this recipe is for medium steak, so adjust it according to your preference.

Hands-On Time: 5 minutes
Cook Time: 6 minutes

Serves 1

- 1 (6-ounce) sirloin steak, cut into 1½" pieces
- 4 button mushrooms, cut into 1½" pieces
- 1 medium zucchini, cut into 1½" pieces
- 1 teaspoon garlic salt
- 1 teaspoon Worcestershire sauce
- 2 tablespoons salted butter, melted

1   Place steak, mushrooms, and zucchini in a medium bowl.

2   In a small bowl, whisk together garlic salt, Worcestershire sauce, and butter. Drizzle over steak and vegetables. Toss to coat all pieces.

3   Place steak and vegetables in air fryer basket. Air fry at 400°F for 3 minutes.

4   Open air fryer and shake to toss. Air fry 3 minutes more.

5   Open air fryer. Using an instant-read thermometer, check to be sure internal temperature of steak is at least 135°F. Remove steak and vegetables from air fryer and serve.

PER SERVING

CALORIES: 604 | **FAT:** 40g | **SODIUM:** 2,289mg | **CARBOHYDRATES:** 10g | **FIBER:** 3g | **SUGAR:** 7g | **PROTEIN:** 41g

Stuffed Pork Chop

This air fryer Stuffed Pork Chop is an amazingly quick and easy meal that goes great with a simple side of vegetables such as the Roasted Asparagus in Chapter 4. The stuffing is a wonderful bite of fall with diced apples, mushrooms, celery, and a savory bread mixture. It has all the wonderful aromas of your favorite holiday stuffing.

Hands-On Time: 15 minutes
Cook Time: 8 minutes

Serves 1

- 2 tablespoons salted butter
- ¼ cup diced yellow onion
- ½ medium celery stalk, diced
- ¼ medium green apple, peeled and diced
- 2 button mushrooms, sliced
- ⅛ teaspoon poultry seasoning
- ¼ teaspoon ground sage
- ¼ teaspoon ground thyme
- ⅛ teaspoon salt
- ⅛ teaspoon ground black pepper
- 1 (¾"-thick) slice white bread, cut into cubes
- 2 tablespoons water
- 1 (1"-thick, 6-ounce) bone-in pork chop
- 1 tablespoon Dijon mustard

1 Melt butter in a small skillet over medium heat. Add onion, celery, apple, and mushrooms to skillet. Sauté until all softened, stirring frequently.

2 Remove from heat. Add poultry seasoning, sage, thyme, salt, and pepper and stir. Add bread cubes and stir. Drizzle in water and stir until stuffing sticks together. Set aside.

3 Using a boning knife, cut a deep pocket in pork chop, cutting close to bone. Using your hands, fill pocket with stuffing mixture. Push stuffing mixture into pocket and pull top of chop over stuffing.

4 Brush top of chop with mustard and spritz with olive oil spray. Place chop in air fryer basket and air fry at 375°F for 8 minutes. Using an instant-read thermometer, check to be sure internal temperature of chop is 145°F.

5 Remove pork chop and let rest 5 minutes before serving.

BONE-IN VERSUS BONELESS

This recipe recommends bone-in chops because the bone provides additional flavor and fat to the meal. However, boneless chops also work with this recipe. Do not cut all the way through so you truly have a pocket for the stuffing. Check internal temperature at 6 minutes for boneless chops.

PER SERVING

CALORIES: 793 | **FAT:** 46g | **SODIUM:** 797mg | **CARBOHYDRATES:** 29g | **FIBER:** 3g | **SUGAR:** 9g | **PROTEIN:** 58g

Breaded Pork Loin Sandwich

This breaded pork sandwich is a great substitute for your favorite state fair food! You can experiment with toppings that you don't typically get at the fair and flavor this sandwich however you'd like! Plus, dinner is on the table in just 15 minutes.

Hands-On Time: 5 minutes
Cook Time: 10 minutes

Serves 1

- ¼ cup all-purpose flour
- ½ teaspoon salt, divided
- ½ teaspoon ground black pepper, divided
- 1 large egg, lightly beaten
- ½ cup panko bread crumbs
- 1 (6-ounce) boneless pork chop, pounded to ¼" thickness
- 1 hamburger bun

1 Prepare breading station with three medium dishes. Mix flour, ¼ teaspoon salt, and ¼ teaspoon pepper with a fork in the first dish. Place egg in the second dish. Mix panko, remaining ¼ teaspoon salt, and remaining ¼ teaspoon pepper with a fork in the third dish. Dredge both sides of pork chop in flour, then egg, and then panko.

2 Gently place chop in air fryer. Spritz top of chop with olive oil spray. Air fry at 400°F for 5 minutes.

3 Open air fryer, flip chop, and spritz again with olive oil spray. Air fry 5 minutes more.

4 Remove from air fryer and serve on bun.

PER SERVING

CALORIES: 691 | FAT: 20g | SODIUM: 1,473mg | CARBOHYDRATES: 54g | FIBER: 1g | SUGAR: 4g | PROTEIN: 67g

Meatball Parmesan Hero Sandwich

A meatball Parmesan hero sandwich is a comforting, cheesy, and hearty classic. It gives you the warm, cozy feel of home. Using premade frozen meatballs is a great way to make this sandwich easier.

Hands-On Time: 5 minutes
Cook Time: 12 minutes

Serves 1

⅓ cup jarred marinara sauce
6 frozen meatballs (3 ounces total)
1 hoagie bun
3 (1-ounce) slices fresh mozzarella
2 tablespoons grated Parmesan cheese

1 Pour marinara into a small oven-safe dish. Place dish and meatballs in air fryer basket. Air fry at 350°F for 5 minutes.

2 Using pot holder, remove dish with marinara. Transfer meatballs to a small plate.

3 Spray tray in air fryer basket with nonstick cooking spray. Place hoagie bun open-side up in air fryer basket. Spread 3 tablespoons warmed marinara on each side of bun. Place meatballs on top of sauce. Lay mozzarella slices on top of meatballs and sprinkle grated Parmesan on top of mozzarella. Close air fryer and air fry at 350°F for 7 minutes.

4 Remove from air fryer, top with remaining marinara, and serve.

PER SERVING

CALORIES: 576 | **FAT:** 30g | **SODIUM:** 1,230mg | **CARBOHYDRATES:** 48g | **FIBER:** 5g | **SUGAR:** 9g | **PROTEIN:** 28g

Pizza Bagels

You may remember those tiny little frozen pizza bagels you had for a snack when you were a kid, but this recipe makes better ones! Making grown-up pizza bagels from scratch is super simple. It's a fun way to have a mini pizza loaded with pepperoni and mushrooms all for yourself.

Hands-On Time: 2 minutes
Cook Time: 8 minutes

Serves 1

1 (4-ounce) bagel
2 tablespoons pizza sauce
8 slices pepperoni
1 button mushroom, sliced
¼ teaspoon Italian seasoning
¼ cup shredded mozzarella cheese

1 Cut bagel in half and place cut-side up in air fryer. Spritz bagel lightly with olive oil spray.

2 Top bagel with pizza sauce, pepperoni, mushroom, Italian seasoning, and mozzarella. Air fry at 350°F for 8 minutes. Using a lower temperature will prevent toppings from blowing off of bagel. Check bagel after 2 minutes to carefully reapply any toppings that may have moved.

3 Using a spatula, remove pizzas from air fryer and serve.

PER SERVING

CALORIES: 452 | **FAT:** 11g | **SODIUM:** 1,096mg | **CARBOHYDRATES:** 61g | **FIBER:** 3g | **SUGAR:** 2g | **PROTEIN:** 21g

Beef and Cheddar Sliders

Sliders are typically a party food, but who says you can't have sliders at home? These Beef and Cheddar Sliders will make any night a party night, and they are easy to prepare. This is how you take a regular deli sandwich and make it a gourmet meal!

Hands-On Time: 5 minutes
Cook Time: 7 minutes

Serves 1

- **4 Hawaiian rolls, sliced in half**
- **3 (1-ounce) slices deli roast beef**
- **1 tablespoon horseradish sauce**
- **1 tablespoon barbecue sauce**
- **2 (1-ounce) slices sharp Cheddar cheese**
- **1 tablespoon salted butter, melted**
- **½ teaspoon light brown sugar**
- **½ teaspoon Dijon mustard**
- **½ teaspoon Worcestershire sauce**

1 Spray a small 6" cake pan with nonstick cooking spray. Lay bottom halves of rolls in pan. Layer rolls with roast beef, horseradish sauce, barbecue sauce, and Cheddar.

2 Place pan in air fryer with rolls open-faced. Air fry at 350°F for 3 minutes.

3 In a small bowl, whisk butter, sugar, mustard, and Worcestershire sauce.

4 Open air fryer and cover sliders with top halves of rolls. Using a basting brush, brush tops of rolls with butter mixture. Air fry 4 minutes more.

5 Using pot holders, remove pan from air fryer. Serve.

PER SERVING

CALORIES: 889 | **FAT:** 44g | **SODIUM:** 1,763mg | **CARBOHYDRATES:** 76g | **FIBER:** 0g | **SUGAR:** 29g | **PROTEIN:** 42g

Pulled Pork Pizza

If you have leftover pulled pork from a cookout, or even precooked store-bought pulled pork, this is a great way to use it up. Feel free to substitute pulled chicken for the pulled pork if you want a lighter flavor. Add red onion for crunch and barbecue sauce for robust taste to make it a delicious meal in minutes.

Hands-On Time: 5 minutes
Cook Time: 5 minutes

Serves 1

¼ cup barbecue sauce, divided
½ cup pulled pork (without sauce)
1 (50-gram) mini naan bread
⅓ cup shredded mozzarella cheese
¼ cup diced red onion

1   In a medium bowl, combine 2 tablespoons barbecue sauce with pork. If pork is cold, microwave 1 minute to loosen it up.

2   Top naan with remaining 2 tablespoons barbecue sauce, pork, mozzarella, and onion.

3   Place naan pizza in air fryer basket. Air fry at 400°F for 5 minutes. Remove from air fryer and serve.

PER SERVING

CALORIES: 583 | FAT: 23g | SODIUM: 1,209mg | CARBOHYDRATES: 60g | FIBER: 2g | SUGAR: 28g | PROTEIN: 28g

Garlic Brown Sugar Pork Chops

Pork chops are an easy choice for an affordable weeknight dinner. In the air fryer, they are juicy and delicious. You'll never eat a dry pork chop again! These pork chops are coated with a thick brown sugar and honey glaze with a nice punch of garlic and herbs.

Hands-On Time: 5 minutes
Cook Time: 8 minutes

Serves 1

- 1 (6-ounce) bone-in pork chop
- 1/16 teaspoon salt
- 1/16 teaspoon ground black pepper
- 2 tablespoons salted butter, melted
- 1 teaspoon minced garlic
- 2 tablespoons light brown sugar
- 1 teaspoon honey
- 1/2 teaspoon Italian seasoning

1 Season pork chop with salt and pepper on both sides. Place chop in air fryer basket. Air fry at 375°F for 2 minutes.

2 Open air fryer and flip chop. Air fry 2 minutes more.

3 In a small bowl, whisk butter, garlic, sugar, honey, and Italian seasoning.

4 Open air fryer and, using a basting brush, brush chop with butter mixture. Air fry at 370°F for 2 minutes.

5 Open air fryer and flip chop. Air fry 2 minutes more. Using an instant-read thermometer, check to be sure internal temperature of chop is 145°F. If pork chop is not up to temperature, air fry 2 minutes more.

6 Remove from air fryer and serve.

PER SERVING

CALORIES: 594 | **FAT:** 30g | **SODIUM:** 437mg | **CARBOHYDRATES:** 34g | **FIBER:** 0g | **SUGAR:** 33g | **PROTEIN:** 34g

Pulled Pork Empanada

An empanada is basically a sandwich pocket stuffed with your choice of fillings. If you were making empanadas for a crowd, you would use puff pastry. But when cooking for one, you can take a shortcut that still makes a delicious empanada. Stuffed with pulled pork and coleslaw, it's a dish you will be making weekly!

Hands-On Time: 5 minutes
Cook Time: 7 minutes

Serves 1

¼ cup pulled pork
2 (¾"-thick) slices white bread, flattened with a rolling pin
2 tablespoons barbecue sauce
2 tablespoons coleslaw
1 large egg, beaten

ALTERNATIVE FILLINGS

If you don't have any coleslaw on hand, you can pair pulled pork with an apple slice or leftover apple pie filling. You could also choose to add shredded Gouda to the pulled pork for a cheesy bite!

1 Place pork in a small microwave-safe bowl and microwave 45 seconds.

2 Lay flattened bread slices on cutting board. Spread pork on bottom half of each bread slice. Top pork with barbecue sauce and coleslaw. Fold bread slices over pork and, using a fork, seal the edges. Using a pastry brush, lightly brush egg onto sealed empanadas.

3 Open air fryer and lightly spray tray with nonstick cooking spray. Place empanadas in air fryer and air fry at 350°F for 6 minutes.

4 Using a spatula, carefully remove empanadas from air fryer and serve.

PER SERVING

CALORIES: 361 | **FAT:** 9g | **SODIUM:** 840mg | **CARBOHYDRATES:** 50g | **FIBER:** 3g | **SUGAR:** 16g | **PROTEIN:** 18g

Philly Cheesesteak Wrap

This Philly Cheesesteak Wrap is an easy way to make a fast-food style wrap in minutes! This wrap is filled with roast beef, cheese, vegetables, and a touch of ranch dressing. The American cheese is reminiscent of the super-gooey cheese sauce of a traditional cheesesteak. You'll want to make this every day!

Hands-On Time: 5 minutes
Cook Time: 5 minutes

Serves 1

- 1 (6") low-carb flour tortilla
- 2 (1-ounce) slices deli roast beef
- 1 (1-ounce) slice American cheese
- 1 button mushroom, sliced
- 1 mini sweet pepper, sliced
- 1 (1"-thick) slice white onion, halved, rings separated
- 1 tablespoon ranch dressing

1 On a cutting board, top tortilla with roast beef, cheese, mushroom, pepper, and onion. Drizzle with ranch dressing. Tightly roll tortilla, leaving ends open.

2 Lay wrap seam-side down in air fryer basket and spritz with olive oil spray. Lay a butter knife on top of wrap to hold it in place. Air fry at 380°F for 5 minutes.

3 Using tongs, carefully remove wrap from air fryer and serve.

PER SERVING

CALORIES: 336 | FAT: 14g | SODIUM: 1,255mg | CARBOHYDRATES: 36g | FIBER: 12g | SUGAR: 11g | PROTEIN: 23g

Hot Italian Sub Sandwich

Hot subs are the best with piles of delicious deli meats, melty cheese, and tangy Italian dressing! This sandwich is easy to make at home. Customize it exactly how you like it. Go to a grocery store deli and get ¼ pound of each type of meat so you can have a variety of meats all in one bite.

Hands-On Time: 5 minutes
Cook Time: 12 minutes

Serves 1

2 strips bacon
1 Italian sub roll
2 (1-ounce) slices salami
2 (1-ounce) slices pepperoni
2 (1-ounce) slices shaved ham
2 (1-ounce) slices provolone cheese
1 (½"-thick) slice red onion, halved, rings separated
1 Roma tomato, thinly sliced
2 tablespoons spicy Italian dressing
1 teaspoon Italian seasoning
¹⁄₁₆ teaspoon salt
¹⁄₁₆ teaspoon ground black pepper

1 Place bacon in air fryer. Air fry at 350°F for 7 minutes. Check bacon. If you prefer bacon crispier, air fry 1–2 minutes more.

2 While bacon is cooking, open sub roll and layer meats and provolone on roll. Place half of meats and provolone on each side so sandwich can evenly heat and cheese can melt.

3 Remove bacon from air fryer and place on a paper towel. Add open-faced sandwich to air fryer. Air fry for 5 minutes until cheese is melted and bubbly.

4 Remove sandwich from air fryer. Top with bacon, onion, tomato, Italian dressing, Italian seasoning, salt, and pepper. Serve.

PER SERVING

CALORIES: 1,137 | FAT: 67g | SODIUM: 4,193mg | CARBOHYDRATES: 55g | FIBER: 3g | SUGAR: 11g | PROTEIN: 65g

Cheeseburger Onion Rings

Everybody loves cheeseburgers and onion rings. They are the ultimate match in pub food! This recipe combines these two foods into one delicious handheld treat! You're basically wrapping a cheeseburger around an onion and then breading and air frying it like an onion ring. This recipe includes a flavorful dipping sauce to top it all off.

Hands-On Time: 15 minutes
Cook Time: 10 minutes

Serves 1

Cheeseburger Onion Rings
1 (1"-thick) slice sweet onion
⅓ pound 80/20 ground beef
⅓ cup sharp Cheddar cheese
⅓ cup all-purpose flour
½ teaspoon chili powder
½ teaspoon coarse sea salt
1 large egg
1 tablespoon water
¾ cup panko bread crumbs

Dipping Sauce
1 tablespoon mayonnaise
1 tablespoon ketchup
½ teaspoon seasoning salt

1 To make Cheeseburger Onion Rings: Separate onion slice into 3 rings. In a medium bowl, mix together beef and Cheddar.

2 Lay onion rings on a cutting board. Wrap and form beef mixture entirely around rings. Turn rings over and add beef to underside, sealing beef completely around onion.

3 Prepare breading station with three medium dishes. Mix flour, chili powder, and salt in the first dish. Beat egg and water in the second dish. Spread panko in the third dish. Roll rings in flour, making sure all sides are coated evenly. Dip flour-coated rings into egg and then into panko until completely coated.

4 Place rings in air fryer basket. Spritz lightly with olive oil spray. Air fry at 370°F for 5 minutes.

5 Open air fryer, flip rings, and spritz again with olive oil spray. Air fry 5 minutes more.

6 To make Dipping Sauce: While Cheeseburger Onion Rings are finishing, mix mayonnaise, ketchup, and seasoning salt.

7 Remove rings from air fryer and serve with Dipping Sauce.

PER SERVING

CALORIES: 761 | **FAT:** 39g | **SODIUM:** 1,937mg | **CARBOHYDRATES:** 48g | **FIBER:** 1g | **SUGAR:** 7g | **PROTEIN:** 44g

Pepperoni Pizzadilla

Quesadillas are a delicious and super-easy dish to make in the air fryer! Add your favorite pizza toppings, such as pepperoni and tomato sauce, to make a pizzadilla. Be careful—the local pizza joint might come knocking at your door for the recipe.

Hands-On Time: 3 minutes
Cook Time: 4 minutes

Serves 1

1 (6") low-carb flour tortilla
2 tablespoons pizza sauce
7 slices pepperoni
¼ cup shredded mozzarella cheese
1⁄16 teaspoon Italian seasoning

1 Lay tortilla on cutting board. Spoon pizza sauce across entire tortilla. Add pepperoni, mozzarella, and Italian seasoning on half of tortilla.

2 Fold tortilla over and place in air fryer basket. Spritz top of tortilla with olive oil spray. Lay a butter knife on top of tortilla to keep it folded over. Air fry at 370°F for 4 minutes until cheese is melted and bubbly.

3 Remove pizzadilla from air fryer, cut into thirds, and serve.

PER SERVING

CALORIES: 221 | **FAT:** 12g | **SODIUM:** 751mg | **CARBOHYDRATES:** 19g | **FIBER:** 10g | **SUGAR:** 2g | **PROTEIN:** 14g

Seafood and Fish

Seafood and fish are versatile, healthy options for dinner. There's a reason they're such a staple in the Mediterranean diet. Whether you're a fan of shellfish like crab, shrimp, and lobster or you prefer your seafood to have fins, this chapter provides you unique and delicious dinner ideas for one.

Breading fish or other seafood is a great basic technique that you can easily learn for many of these recipes. Enjoy breaded entrées on their own, in salads, or in tacos. Look back to your childhood with the Homemade Fish Sticks. Of course, elevating an evening meal with seafood is easy to do too. You can make a fancier dinner like Crab-Stuffed Mahi-Mahi, perfect with a glass of white wine, or even air fryer Lobster Tail.

Bacon-Wrapped Scallops

Scallops wrapped in bacon are a decadent dinner. This recipe brings the sweetness from sea scallops together with the savory saltiness of bacon. You'll be surprised how easy and fast the air fryer makes this dish, and it's great as an appetizer or a main course.

Hands-On Time: 2 minutes
Cook Time: 8 minutes

Serves 1

2 strips bacon, cut in half
4 large sea scallops
¼ cup barbecue sauce

REMOVING SIDE MUSCLE ON SCALLOPS
The side muscle on a scallop is edible, but it's tough and not as sweet. The muscle is a little rectangular piece of tissue on the side of the large sea scallop. Pinch the muscle between your thumb and finger and you can pull it right off.

1 Place bacon in air fryer basket and air fry at 400°F for 3 minutes.

2 Pull off scallops' muscles. Open air fryer and remove bacon. Wrap each scallop in ½ strip of bacon and secure with a toothpick.

3 Place bacon-wrapped scallops in air fryer basket. Lightly brush with barbecue sauce. Air fry at 400°F for 5 minutes until scallop is tender and opaque and bacon is cooked through.

4 Using tongs, remove scallops from air fryer and serve.

PER SERVING

CALORIES: 249 | **FAT:** 6g | **SODIUM:** 1,293mg | **CARBOHYDRATES:** 31g | **FIBER:** 1g | **SUGAR:** 24g | **PROTEIN:** 15g

Scallops with Lemony Garlic Butter

These Scallops with Lemony Garlic Butter are ready in minutes. This dish is a delicious way to eat scallops. The scallops' sweetness is made just a little better with the addition of butter, garlic, capers, and lemon juice.

Hands-On Time: 5 minutes
Cook Time: 6 minutes

Serves 1

- 4 large sea scallops
- ⅛ teaspoon Old Bay Seasoning
- 1 tablespoon salted butter, melted
- ¼ teaspoon lemon juice
- ¼ teaspoon minced garlic
- ½ teaspoon capers

1 Pull off scallops' muscles. Season scallops on both sides with Old Bay Seasoning.

2 In a small bowl, whisk butter, lemon juice, garlic, and capers until well combined.

3 Dip each scallop in butter mixture, then place in air fryer basket. Air fry at 400°F for 6 minutes until scallops are tender and opaque.

4 Remove scallops and pour remaining butter mixture over scallops, reheating butter mixture for 15 seconds if needed. Serve.

PER SERVING

CALORIES: 143 | FAT: 11g | SODIUM: 429mg | CARBOHYDRATES: 2g | FIBER: 0g | SUGAR: 0g | PROTEIN: 7g

Lobster Tail

This air fryer Lobster Tail will remind you that cooking for one doesn't mean you can't have a fancy dinner! Snip the lobster tail with scissors, add a little butter and garlic, air fry, and done. This decadent meal is on the table in 12 minutes. If you need to defrost your lobster tail, put it in a zip-top bag, squeeze out the air, and place the bag in cold water for 30 minutes.

Hands-On Time: 5 minutes
Cook Time: 7 minutes

Serves 1

1 (4-ounce) lobster tail
2 tablespoons salted butter
½ teaspoon coarse sea salt
1 teaspoon minced garlic
1 lemon wedge

1   Butterfly lobster tail by cutting through shell to tail. Do not cut through tail. Pull apart shell to expose lobster meat. You may need to break off pieces of shell to open it up.

2   Place butter, salt, and garlic in a small microwave-safe bowl and microwave 35 seconds. Remove from microwave and whisk to combine. Pour half of the garlic butter into a smaller container for when you serve the dish.

3   Place lobster tail open-side up in air fryer basket. Use garlic butter in microwavable container to baste. Air fry at 360°F for 3 minutes.

4   Open air fryer and baste again. Air fry 3 minutes more.

5   Remove tail from air fryer, open shell with your fingers, and pull out lobster meat. Meat is still attached at base of tail, but you can easily slip your fingers underneath and pull it out.

6   Serve with remaining garlic butter and lemon wedge.

PER SERVING

CALORIES: 241 | **FAT:** 22g | **SODIUM:** 1,333mg | **CARBOHYDRATES:** 1g | **FIBER:** 0g | **SUGAR:** 0g | **PROTEIN:** 8g

Crunchy Salmon Nuggets

Crunchy Salmon Nuggets are fun and delicious! Plus, you can dip them in this recipe's quick Greek tzatziki sauce. Perfect as an appetizer or entrée, it's on the table in about 15 minutes. Breading salmon in panko adds a nice crunch. You can substitute Italian seasoning if you do not have a Greek seasoning blend.

Hands-On Time: 10 minutes
Cook Time: 6 minutes

Serves 1

Tzatziki Sauce

¼ cup nonfat plain Greek yogurt
2 tablespoons grated cucumber
½ teaspoon minced garlic
½ teaspoon dill
⅟₁₆ teaspoon coarse sea salt

Salmon

2 large egg whites, beaten
½ cup panko bread crumbs
1 tablespoon Greek seasoning
1 (8-ounce) skinless thick-cut salmon fillet, cut into 1½" pieces

1 For Tzatziki Sauce: Combine all ingredients in a small bowl and refrigerate until serving.

2 For Salmon: Prepare breading station with two medium dishes. Place egg whites in the first dish. Mix panko and Greek seasoning in the second dish. Lightly dip Salmon pieces into egg whites, letting excess drip off. Then coat Salmon in panko mixture and shake off excess.

3 Place Salmon pieces in air fryer basket and spritz with olive oil spray. Air fry at 350°F for 3 minutes.

4 Open air fryer, flip Salmon pieces, and spritz again with olive oil spray. Air fry 3 minutes more.

5 Remove Salmon from air fryer and serve with Tzatziki Sauce.

PER SERVING

CALORIES: 505 | **FAT:** 14g | **SODIUM:** 3,259mg | **CARBOHYDRATES:** 30g | **FIBER:** 0g | **SUGAR:** 3g | **PROTEIN:** 58g

Crab Cakes

Crab cakes are always a favorite as an appetizer, but they also make a delicious dinner. The best thing about making them at home is that you can use good quality crabmeat and a lot of it! You'll have big pieces of crab in every bite, along with Dijon mustard, dill, and lemon juice. Plus, they're fast and easy to make! Serve these on greens for a healthy, filling dinner.

Hands-On Time: 10 minutes
Cook Time: 8 minutes

Serves 1

Crab Cakes

4 ounces jumbo lump crabmeat
1 large egg yolk
2 tablespoons mayonnaise
2 tablespoons bread crumbs
1 tablespoon Dijon mustard
½ teaspoon dried dill
½ teaspoon Worcestershire sauce
¼ teaspoon lemon juice
⅛ teaspoon hot sauce
¼ teaspoon salt
⅛ teaspoon ground black pepper

Crab Cake Sauce

1 tablespoon mayonnaise
¼ teaspoon lemon juice
⅛ teaspoon hot sauce
1/16 teaspoon coarse sea salt

CRABMEAT OPTIONS

Avoid using imitation crab. Canned is cheapest, but it's stringy and lacks flavor and substance. In your grocery's seafood section, you can find jumbo lump or wild-caught white crabmeat. Both of these work great. You may also use ½ cup fresh crabmeat.

1 To make Crab Cakes: In a medium bowl, delicately mix all ingredients.

2 Lay a sheet of parchment paper that fits into your air fryer on a cutting board. Set a 2½" round cookie cutter on the parchment. Spoon half of crab mixture into cookie cutter, press lightly, and form cake. Remove cookie cutter from cake and repeat to make second cake.

3 Carefully pick up parchment with cakes on it and place in air fryer basket. Spritz cakes with olive oil spray and air fry at 375°F for 4 minutes.

4 Open air fryer, flip cakes, and spritz again with olive oil spray. Air fry 4 minutes more.

5 To make Crab Cake Sauce: While cakes are frying, combine all ingredients in a small bowl.

6 Remove Crab Cakes from air fryer and serve with Crab Cake Sauce.

PER SERVING

CALORIES: 514 | FAT: 37g | SODIUM: 2,149mg | CARBOHYDRATES: 13g | FIBER: 1g | SUGAR: 2g | PROTEIN: 27g

Bang Bang Shrimp

You can eat these shrimp on their own or pop them into tortillas with avocado to make tacos. The dish is easy to make and a little messy, which is the fun part! Sweet Thai chili sauce and gochujang make up the sauce—you may want to double the sauce recipe so you have extra for dipping.

Hands-On Time: 10 minutes
Cook Time: 5 minutes

Serves 1

Shrimp
¼ cup all-purpose flour
1 teaspoon salt
½ teaspoon ground black pepper
1 large egg
¼ cup buttermilk
2 tablespoons cornstarch
½ cup panko bread crumbs
6 raw extra-large shrimp, peeled and deveined

Sauce
2 tablespoons mayonnaise
2 tablespoons sweet Thai chili sauce
1 tablespoon gochujang Korean chili sauce
1 tablespoon sliced green onion

1 To make Shrimp: Prepare breading station with three medium dishes. Mix flour, salt, and pepper in the first dish. Beat egg and buttermilk in the second dish. Mix cornstarch and panko in the third dish.

2 Bread Shrimp by dipping into flour, then egg, and then panko, coating all sides.

3 Place breaded Shrimp in air fryer basket and spritz with olive oil spray. Air fry at 400°F for 2 minutes. Open air fryer, carefully flip Shrimp with tongs, and spritz again with olive oil spray. Air fry 2 minutes more.

4 To make Sauce: While Shrimp are cooking, whisk all ingredients except green onion together in a small bowl.

5 When Shrimp are done, carefully remove with tongs and dip in Sauce. Air fry 1–2 minutes more.

6 Carefully remove Shrimp from air fryer. Sprinkle with green onion and serve with remaining Sauce.

PER SERVING

CALORIES: 602 | **FAT:** 28g | **SODIUM:** 2,370mg | **CARBOHYDRATES:** 67g | **FIBER:** 2g | **SUGAR:** 25g | **PROTEIN:** 17g

Shrimp Louie Salad

Shrimp Louie Salad originated on the West Coast in the early 1900s. It's made with shrimp, lettuce, egg, avocado, and juicy tomatoes. The dressing is similar to Thousand Island dressing. You will also find that people substitute crab for the shrimp to make a Crab Louie Salad.

Hands-On Time: 10 minutes
Cook Time: 7 minutes

Serves 1

Dressing
2 tablespoons mayonnaise
1 tablespoon ketchup
1 tablespoon chili sauce
1 teaspoon dried minced onion
1/16 teaspoon coarse sea salt
1/2 teaspoon Worcestershire sauce

Shrimp Salad
9 raw large shrimp, peeled, deveined, and tails removed
1 tablespoon olive oil
2 teaspoons Old Bay Seasoning
1/2 head romaine lettuce
1/2 small tomato, diced
1/2 medium ripe avocado, pitted, peeled, and sliced
1 hard-boiled large egg

1 To make Dressing: In a small bowl, whisk together all ingredients. Refrigerate until ready to serve.

2 To make Shrimp Salad: In a small bowl, toss shrimp with oil and Old Bay Seasoning.

3 Place shrimp in air fryer basket and air fry at 400°F for 7 minutes.

4 Tear romaine into pieces, place in a medium bowl, and drizzle Dressing on top. Top with tomato, shrimp, avocado, and egg.

PER SERVING

CALORIES: 634 | FAT: 48g | SODIUM: 2,101mg | CARBOHYDRATES: 26g | FIBER: 12g | SUGAR: 11g | PROTEIN: 22g

HARD-BOILED EGGS

Look for the full recipe in Chapter 2, but here's a condensed version: Place egg in air fryer and air fry at 250°F for 15 minutes. Place in ice bath for a few minutes to cool. Peel and add to the salad as instructed.

Salmon Patties

These Salmon Patties will make you forget the ones you had growing up. Replacing that old-fashioned canned salmon with higher-quality salmon is the first step to making these elevated patties. Adding peppers, dill, Worcestershire sauce, lemon, and more makes them even tastier.

Hands-On Time: 10 minutes
Cook Time: 10 minutes

Serves 1

- 1 (4-ounce) pouch pink salmon in olive oil
- 1 large egg
- 1 mini sweet pepper, finely diced
- 2 tablespoons bread crumbs
- 2 tablespoons all-purpose flour
- ½ teaspoon Worcestershire sauce
- ½ teaspoon lemon juice
- ¼ teaspoon dried dill
- ¼ teaspoon minced garlic
- 1⁄16 teaspoon coarse sea salt
- 1⁄16 teaspoon ground black pepper

SALMON OPTIONS

There are many varieties of salmon to choose from. The best option is fresh salmon. If cooking fresh, slightly undercook the salmon because it will continue cooking as you air fry. Pouched salmon is higher quality and more flavorful than canned and makes a fabulous second choice.

1 Place all ingredients in a medium bowl and mix with a fork until well combined.

2 Lay a sheet of parchment paper that fits into your air fryer on a cutting board. Set a 2½" round cookie cutter on the parchment. Spoon half of salmon mixture into cookie cutter, press lightly, and form patty. Remove cookie cutter from patty and repeat to make second patty.

3 Carefully pick up parchment with patties on it and place in air fryer basket. Spritz patties with olive oil spray and air fry at 380°F for 5 minutes.

4 Open air fryer, flip patties, and spritz again with olive oil spray. Air fry 5 minutes more. Remove patties from air fryer and serve.

PER SERVING

CALORIES: 298 | FAT: 7g | SODIUM: 546mg | CARBOHYDRATES: 26g | FIBER: 1g | SUGAR: 2g | PROTEIN: 33g

Cilantro Lime–Breaded Shrimp

Air fryer shrimp are the best! They cook so quickly and are very crunchy. Plus, adding fresh cilantro and lime zest will make your shrimp zingy and packed with flavor. These Cilantro Lime–Breaded Shrimp are great on their own, dipped into spicy ranch, or added to tortillas with cabbage and avocado for simple shrimp tacos.

Hands-On Time: 10 minutes
Cook Time: 8 minutes

Serves 1

¼ cup all-purpose flour
1 large egg, beaten
1 tablespoon chopped fresh cilantro
½ cup panko bread crumbs
1 small lime
6 raw extra-large shrimp, peeled, deveined, and tails removed

1 Prepare breading station with three medium dishes. Place flour in the first dish, egg in the second dish, and cilantro and panko in the third dish. Zest lime and add zest to dish with panko. Then, juice lime, add lime juice to dish with egg, and whisk together. Dip each shrimp into flour, then egg, and then panko, coating all sides and pressing panko onto shrimp.

2 Spray tray in air fryer basket with nonstick cooking spray. Place shrimp in air fryer basket and spritz shrimp with olive oil spray. Air fry at 350°F for 4 minutes. Open air fryer, flip shrimp, and spritz again with olive oil spray. Air fry 4 minutes more.

3 Remove shrimp and enjoy!

PER SERVING

CALORIES: 228 | **FAT:** 4g | **SODIUM:** 361mg | **CARBOHYDRATES:** 34g | **FIBER:** 1g | **SUGAR:** 1g | **PROTEIN:** 14g

Crunchy Italian Tilapia

This recipe uses a light breading and makes a flavorful, crunchy fish dinner. This dish goes great with the Cheesy Tomato Slices in Chapter 4.

Hands-On Time: 5 minutes
Cook Time: 12 minutes

Serves 1

1 large egg, beaten
¼ cup bread crumbs
1 tablespoon Italian seasoning
¼ teaspoon coarse sea salt
1 (6-ounce) tilapia fillet

1 Prepare breading station with two medium dishes. Place egg in the first dish. Mix bread crumbs, Italian seasoning, and salt in the second dish. Dip tilapia into egg, coating completely. Then coat with bread crumb mixture, pressing crumbs onto tilapia.

2 Spray tray in air fryer basket with nonstick cooking spray. Spritz tilapia with olive oil spray and air fry at 350°F for 12 minutes.

3 Remove tilapia and enjoy!

PER SERVING

CALORIES: 304 | FAT: 6g | SODIUM: 800mg | CARBOHYDRATES: 20g | FIBER: 1g | SUGAR: 2g | PROTEIN: 41g

Shrimp Scampi

Shrimp scampi is a very popular restaurant dish, and this air fryer version is phenomenal. You can also serve this scampi with crusty bread rolls or on top of angel hair pasta.

Hands-On Time: 3 minutes
Cook Time: 9 minutes

Serves 1

9 raw large shrimp, peeled and deveined, tails left on
1⁄16 teaspoon coarse sea salt
1⁄16 teaspoon ground black pepper
1 teaspoon olive oil
2 tablespoons salted butter, softened
1 teaspoon minced garlic
¼ teaspoon Italian seasoning
1 tablespoon grated Parmesan cheese

1 Season shrimp with salt and pepper.

2 Combine oil, butter, and garlic in a small baking dish. Place dish in air fryer basket. Air fry at 400°F for 3 minutes.

3 Once butter is melted, using pot holders, remove dish from air fryer. Add shrimp to the dish and coat with garlic butter. Return dish to air fryer. Air fry 6 minutes more.

4 Using pot holders, remove dish from air fryer and sprinkle shrimp with Italian seasoning and Parmesan. Serve.

PER SERVING

CALORIES: 318 | FAT: 28g | SODIUM: 799mg | CARBOHYDRATES: 2g | FIBER: 0g | SUGAR: 0g | PROTEIN: 12g

Healthy Fish and Chips

Fish and chips are delicious but are usually dripping with grease. Your air fryer is the solution to providing you a healthier version that still has all the crunch! This recipe uses cod, which is a thick white fish, though you may use haddock or flounder instead. If you use haddock, you'll want to reduce the cook time, as it's a thinner fish.

Hands-On Time: 10 minutes
Cook Time: 16 minutes

Serves 1

- 1 small russet potato, scrubbed clean
- 1 tablespoon olive oil
- 1 teaspoon coarse sea salt
- 2 tablespoons all-purpose flour
- 1 teaspoon paprika
- 1 large egg, beaten
- ¼ cup panko bread crumbs
- 1 (8-ounce) cod fillet

1 Slice potato in half and then into ¼"-thick sticks. Rinse sticks with cold water, drain, and pat dry.

2 In a medium bowl, toss potato with oil and salt. Place potato on one side of air fryer basket.

3 Prepare breading station with three medium dishes. Mix flour and paprika in the first dish, place egg in the second dish, and spread panko in the third dish. Dip cod into flour, then egg, and then panko, coating all sides and pressing panko onto cod.

4 Spray empty half of tray in air fryer basket with nonstick cooking spray. Place cod on tray and spritz with olive oil spray. Air fry at 400°F for 8 minutes.

5 Open air fryer, flip fish, and spritz again with olive oil spray. Toss fries. Air fry 8 minutes more.

6 Remove fish and chips and serve.

PER SERVING

CALORIES: 603 | **FAT:** 18g | **SODIUM:** 2,151mg | **CARBOHYDRATES:** 56g | **FIBER:** 4g | **SUGAR:** 3g | **PROTEIN:** 51g

Salmon Oscar

Salmon Oscar is one of the easiest meals, but it looks and tastes super fancy. Seared salmon on top of crunchy asparagus, topped with lump crabmeat and a quick cheater béarnaise sauce. Cooking for one doesn't have to be boring!

Hands-On Time: 2 minutes
Cook Time: 12 minutes

Serves 1

Salmon, Asparagus, and Crab
1 (6-ounce) salmon fillet
¹⁄₁₆ teaspoon ground black pepper
⅛ teaspoon coarse sea salt, divided
¼ pound asparagus, trimmed
2 ounces lump crabmeat, room temperature

Béarnaise Sauce
½ teaspoon lemon juice
1 teaspoon dried minced onion
⅛ teaspoon dried tarragon
2 tablespoons mayonnaise
2 tablespoons 2% milk
½ teaspoon Dijon mustard

1   To make Salmon, Asparagus, and Crab: On a cutting board, season salmon on both sides with ¹⁄₁₆ teaspoon pepper and salt. Place in air fryer basket and air fry at 350°F for 4 minutes.

2   Open air fryer and flip salmon. Add asparagus to air fryer. Spritz with olive oil spray and season with remaining ¹⁄₁₆ teaspoon salt. Air fry 4 minutes more.

3   To make Bearnaise Sauce: While salmon is cooking, combine lemon juice, onion, and tarragon in a small saucepan. Cook over medium heat, stirring, until onion is tender, about 2 minutes. Reduce heat to low and whisk in mayonnaise, milk, and mustard. Stir and heat through 2 minutes more. Remove from heat.

4   Remove asparagus from air fryer and set on a large plate. Top with salmon. Place crabmeat on top of salmon. Pour sauce over crabmeat and enjoy!

PER SERVING

CALORIES: 510 | **FAT:** 31g | **SODIUM:** 886mg | **CARBOHYDRATES:** 5g | **FIBER:** 1g | **SUGAR:** 2g | **PROTEIN:** 47g

Sweet and Spicy–Glazed Salmon

Salmon is one of the healthiest proteins to cook in the air fryer. This recipe adds a complex sweet and spicy taste to the dish that you won't soon forget! You may replace the gochujang sauce with sriracha.

Hands-On Time: 5 minutes
Cook Time: 8 minutes

Serves 1

1 (6-ounce) salmon fillet
1⁄16 teaspoon coarse sea salt
1⁄16 teaspoon ground black pepper
1 teaspoon soy sauce
1 teaspoon honey
½ teaspoon minced garlic
2 teaspoons gochujang Korean chili sauce

1   Season salmon with salt and pepper.

2   In a small bowl, mix soy sauce, honey, garlic, and gochujang.

3   Place salmon in air fryer basket. Baste salmon with honey mixture. Air fry at 360°F for 8 minutes.

4   Remove from air fryer and serve.

PER SERVING

CALORIES: 306 | FAT: 12g | SODIUM: 585mg | CARBOHYDRATES: 11g | FIBER: 1g | SUGAR: 9g | PROTEIN: 35g

COOKING SALMON FROM FROZEN

You can make this recipe with frozen salmon with a few tweaks. Nothing will stick to frozen fish, so place fillet in air fryer and air fry at 350°F for 5 minutes to thaw. Then, baste fish with sauce and air fry 5 minutes more. Your salmon will be perfectly seasoned!

Tuna Melt Wrap

Changing your standard tuna melt into a wrap makes it even easier to eat. Plus, if you're watching your carb intake, you can use a low-carb tortilla. Shredded cheese is used in this wrap because it melts quickly. Serve this Tuna Melt Wrap with the Potato Chips from Chapter 3 and a pickle for a true deli experience at home.

Hands-On Time: 5 minutes
Cook Time: 4 minutes

Serves 1

- 1 (2½-ounce) packet foil-packed tuna
- 1 tablespoon mayonnaise
- 1 tablespoon sliced green onion
- ¼ teaspoon dried parsley
- ½ teaspoon Dijon mustard
- ⅛ teaspoon minced garlic
- ¼ teaspoon lemon juice
- ¹⁄₁₆ teaspoon coarse sea salt
- ¹⁄₁₆ teaspoon ground black pepper
- 1 (6") low-carb flour tortilla
- 2 tablespoons shredded pepper jack cheese

1 In a medium bowl, mix tuna, mayonnaise, green onion, parsley, mustard, garlic, lemon juice, salt, and pepper.

2 On tortilla, lay out tuna salad. Top with pepper jack. Tightly roll tortilla, leaving ends open.

3 Lay wrap seam-side down in air fryer basket and spritz with olive oil spray. Lay a butter knife on top of wrap to keep in it in place. Air fry at 400°F for 4 minutes.

4 Using tongs, carefully remove wrap from air fryer and serve.

PER SERVING

CALORIES: 288 | FAT: 17g | SODIUM: 890mg | CARBOHYDRATES: 16g | FIBER: 9g | SUGAR: 1g | PROTEIN: 25g

Homemade Fish Sticks

Want to elevate your childhood craving? These grown-up fish sticks are made by hand with cod and an easy-to-make breading. You'll never want the frozen ones again. Also included is a quick tartar sauce recipe that makes just enough for dinner!

Hands-On Time: 10 minutes
Cook Time: 8 minutes

Serves 1

Fish Sticks
¼ cup all-purpose flour
½ teaspoon paprika
¼ teaspoon coarse sea salt
¼ teaspoon ground black
    pepper
1 large egg, beaten
½ cup panko bread crumbs
2 tablespoons grated
    Parmesan cheese
1 (6-ounce) cod fillet, sliced
    into 1" × 4" strips

Tartar Sauce
2 tablespoons mayonnaise
1 tablespoon pickle relish
⅛ teaspoon lemon juice
1⁄16 teaspoon salt

1. To make Fish Sticks: Prepare breading station with three medium dishes. Mix flour, paprika, salt, and pepper in the first dish. Place egg in the second dish. Mix panko and Parmesan in the third dish. Dip cod strips into flour and coat completely. Dip floured strips into egg, and then coat with panko mixture, pressing mixture onto cod.

2. Spray tray in air fryer basket with nonstick cooking spray and place strips in basket. Spritz sticks with olive oil spray and air fry at 400°F for 4 minutes.

3. Open air fryer, flip sticks, and spritz again with olive oil spray. Air fry 4 minutes more.

4. To make Tartar Sauce: While Fish Sticks are cooking, combine all ingredients in a small bowl.

5. Remove Fish Sticks from air fryer and serve with Tartar Sauce.

PER SERVING

CALORIES: 552 | **FAT:** 26g | **SODIUM:** 994mg | **CARBOHYDRATES:** 37g | **FIBER:** 1g | **SUGAR:** 1g | **PROTEIN:** 40g

Soy-Marinated Ahi Tuna Steak

A tuna steak cooked to medium-rare or medium is super easy to make. Whip up a delicious and quick marinade of soy sauce, honey, sesame oil, ginger, and more. Pair this with Dijon Parmesan Potatoes from Chapter 4 to have a meal on the table in minutes.

Hands-On Time: 5 minutes
Cook Time: 7 minutes

Serves 1

- 2 tablespoons soy sauce
- 1 teaspoon honey
- ½ teaspoon fresh ginger
- 1 teaspoon sesame oil
- ½ teaspoon mirin
- 1 (4-ounce) boneless, skinless tuna steak
- ¼ teaspoon sesame seeds

INTERNAL TEMPERATURE FOR TUNA

Tuna is best eaten medium-rare or medium. It's best to check the temperature of meat and fish with an instant-read thermometer. For tuna, the temperature ranges are: 110°F–115°F for rare, 125°F–130°F for medium-rare, 135°F–145°F for medium, and over 150°F for well done.

1 In a quart-sized plastic zip-top bag, combine soy sauce, honey, ginger, oil, and mirin. Add tuna, shake it around a little, and seal. Marinate in refrigerator at least 60 minutes.

2 Remove tuna from refrigerator and place in air fryer basket. Air fry at 380°F for 4 minutes.

3 Open air fryer and flip tuna. Air fry 3 minutes more.

4 Remove from air fryer, garnish with sesame seeds, and serve.

PER SERVING

CALORIES: 133 | FAT: 1g | SODIUM: 227mg | CARBOHYDRATES: 1g | FIBER: 0g | SUGAR: 1g | PROTEIN: 28g

Citrus Avocado Fish Tacos

These air fryer fish tacos are going to be a weekly staple. Once marinated, the fish takes no time to make and comes out flaky and perfect. Top it with fresh toppings like avocado, cabbage, and limes. It's light and delicious. The mojo criollo marinade is found in grocery stores in the Mexican food aisle. It's a citrus garlic Cuban marinade that livens up any fish or chicken dish.

Hands-On Time: 5 minutes
Cook Time: 12 minutes

Serves 1

1 (6-ounce) tilapia fillet
½ cup mojo criollo marinade
2 tablespoons ranch dressing
1 teaspoon juice from jar of pickled jalapeños
1 medium lime, quartered, divided
2 (6") low-carb flour tortillas
2 tablespoons queso fresco
¼ cup shredded cabbage
½ medium ripe avocado, pitted, peeled, and sliced
2 tablespoons pico de gallo
1 tablespoon pickled jalapeño slices

1 Place tilapia and marinade in a quart-sized plastic zip-top bag and seal bag. Marinate in refrigerator at least 4 hours.

2 Place tilapia fillet in air fryer basket and air fry at 350°F for 12 minutes.

3 While tilapia is air frying, in a small bowl, mix together ranch dressing, jalapeño juice, and juice of 2 lime wedges. Set aside.

4 Lay tortillas on a large plate. Top with queso fresco. Remove tilapia from air fryer. Shred fish into bite-sized chunks and add to tortilla.

5 Top tacos with cabbage, avocado, pico de gallo, and jalapeño slices and drizzle with jalapeño ranch sauce. Serve with remaining 2 lime wedges.

PER SERVING

CALORIES: 607 | **FAT:** 32g | **SODIUM:** 1,524mg | **CARBOHYDRATES:** 44g | **FIBER:** 23g | **SUGAR:** 6g | **PROTEIN:** 49g

Shrimp Toast

This air fried Shrimp Toast is a fresh take on the popular yet greasy Chinese restaurant appetizer. You'll enjoy this savory, creamy shrimp spread on top of a crispy bagel. This dish is also a little heartier and makes a delicious dinner. Pair it with a side salad for a complete meal.

Hands-On Time: 5 minutes
Cook Time: 6 minutes

Serves 1

4 raw large shrimp, peeled, deveined, and tails removed
1 tablespoon mayonnaise
1 tablespoon salted butter, melted
1 tablespoon full-fat cream cheese, softened
½ teaspoon minced garlic
1 teaspoon thinly sliced green onion
1/16 teaspoon coarse sea salt
1/16 teaspoon ground black pepper
1 (4-ounce) bagel

1   Chop shrimp into small pieces, almost minced.

2   In a medium bowl, mix shrimp, mayonnaise, butter, cream cheese, garlic, green onion, salt, and pepper into a paste.

3   Slice open bagel and spread mixture onto each bagel half. Place in air fryer basket. Air fry at 370°F for 6 minutes.

4   Remove bagel from air fryer and serve.

PER SERVING

CALORIES: 550 | FAT: 26g | SODIUM: 1,045mg | CARBOHYDRATES: 58g | FIBER: 3g | SUGAR: 1g | PROTEIN: 16g

Spinach Artichoke Halibut

Premade spinach artichoke dip is great for more than just dipping—it's a great topping for chicken or fish. Halibut is a surprisingly juicy white fish, and the creaminess of the dip complements the fish nicely. This recipe is also quick, simple, and delicious. If you don't have halibut, this works well with tilapia, salmon, or even a chicken breast!

Hands-On Time: 5 minutes
Cook Time: 12 minutes

Serves 1

- ¹⁄₁₆ teaspoon coarse sea salt
- ¹⁄₁₆ teaspoon ground black pepper
- 1 (6-ounce) halibut fillet
- 3 tablespoons spinach artichoke dip

1 Sprinkle salt and pepper on halibut and place halibut in air fryer basket. Air fry at 370°F for 6 minutes.

2 Open air fryer and spoon dip onto fish, pressing down so dip covers entire fillet. Air fry 6 minutes more.

3 Remove halibut from air fryer and serve.

PER SERVING

CALORIES: 229 | FAT: 9g | SODIUM: 550mg | CARBOHYDRATES: 2g | FIBER: 0g | SUGAR: 0g | PROTEIN: 35g

Cajun Shrimp and Vegetables

Spicy Cajun Shrimp and Vegetables is a delicious all-in-one meal. When cooking for one, grab a cup of microwavable rice and your dinner is made. Yellow squash, sweet peppers, and onion add a lot of texture and crunch to this shrimp dish. If you like it spicier, add a little more Cajun seasoning.

Hands-On Time: 5 minutes
Cook Time: 7 minutes

Serves 1

- **9 raw large shrimp, peeled, deveined, and tails removed**
- **1 small yellow squash, sliced into half-moons**
- **2 mini sweet peppers, cut into 1" chunks**
- **½ small yellow onion, cut into ½" chunks**
- **2 teaspoons olive oil**
- **1 teaspoon Cajun seasoning**
- **4 ounces microwavable brown rice**

1 In a large bowl, combine shrimp, squash, peppers, onion, oil, and seasoning and toss to coat.

2 Place shrimp and vegetables in air fryer basket. Air fry at 400°F for 4 minutes.

3 While shrimp and vegetables are air frying, heat rice in microwave according to package directions.

4 Open air fryer and toss contents. Air fry 3 minutes more.

5 Spoon rice onto large plate and top with shrimp and vegetables. Serve.

PER SERVING

CALORIES: 341 | **FAT:** 12g | **SODIUM:** 652mg | **CARBOHYDRATES:** 43g | **FIBER:** 3g | **SUGAR:** 6g | **PROTEIN:** 15g

Crab-Stuffed Mahi-Mahi

In this recipe, mahi-mahi is stuffed with a creamy crab filling and topped with a lemon-butter sauce. Plus, it's ready in about 15 minutes. Feel free to substitute any thin, flaky white fish, such as tilapia, perch, or flounder. This dish pairs perfectly with Carrot Fries from Chapter 4.

Hands-On Time: 8 minutes
Cook Time: 9 minutes

Serves 1

- 1 (4-ounce) mahi-mahi fillet
- ⅙ teaspoon coarse sea salt
- ⅙ teaspoon ground black pepper
- 2 tablespoons full-fat cream cheese, softened
- ¼ teaspoon lemon-herb seasoning
- ¼ teaspoon minced garlic
- 3 tablespoons lump crabmeat
- 1 tablespoon salted butter, melted
- 1 teaspoon lemon juice

1 Place mahi-mahi on a cutting board, sprinkle with salt and pepper, and, with your fingers, press fillet to flatten to about ¾" thickness.

2 In a small bowl, mix cream cheese, lemon-herb seasoning, and garlic. Fold in crabmeat gently, so as not to break it up. Spread cream cheese mixture onto mahi-mahi.

3 Roll up fish fillet and place fish roll seam-side down in air fryer. Air fry at 370°F for 5 minutes.

4 In a small bowl, mix butter and lemon juice. Open air fryer and baste fish roll with some of lemon butter. Air fry 4 minutes more.

5 Remove roll from air fryer and serve with remaining lemon butter.

PER SERVING

CALORIES: 323 | **FAT:** 20g | **SODIUM:** 748mg | **CARBOHYDRATES:** 2g | **FIBER:** 0g | **SUGAR:** 1g | **PROTEIN:** 28g

8

Vegetarian

Looking for some meatless options for your air fryer? Whether you only observe Meatless Mondays or you're a strict full-time vegetarian, this chapter has a lot of options for you. Because they use whole foods and single-portion products, these recipes are also budget-friendly. Plus, if you're really hungry, some of these dishes pair nicely with each other or with meat dishes in this book. Looking for a light lunch? Try the Zucchini Lasagna Roll-Ups or the Crunchy Tofu Nuggets. If you're searching for something a little more substantial, try the Roasted Cauliflower Steak with Chimichurri Sauce or the Mushroom Burger.

This chapter draws inspiration from many cultures and will be a well-rounded section, whether you're cooking for yourself or for a vegetarian guest. Let's get cooking!

Spinach, Tomato, and Mushroom Quesadilla

Quesadillas are an easy, cheesy air fryer meal! Incorporating multiple vegetables, like mushrooms, spinach, and tomatoes, alongside the cheese adds texture and depth to your quesadilla. The spinach can easily be swapped with kale, and you could also use sun-dried tomatoes instead of regular tomatoes for extra flavor.

Hands-On Time: 8 minutes
Cook Time: 10 minutes

Serves 1

- 3 button mushrooms, sliced
- 4 cherry tomatoes, sliced
- 2 ounces baby spinach, torn into small pieces
- 1 tablespoon olive oil
- 1⁄16 teaspoon coarse sea salt
- 1⁄16 teaspoon ground black pepper
- 1 (6") low-carb flour tortilla
- 1⁄4 cup shredded mozzarella cheese

1 In a small baking dish, combine mushrooms, tomatoes, spinach, oil, salt, and pepper. Place dish in air fryer basket and air fry at 370°F for 5 minutes.

2 Lay tortilla on a cutting board. Add mozzarella along half of tortilla. Open air fryer and, using pot holders, remove dish. Spoon vegetables onto mozzarella.

3 Spray air fryer tray with nonstick cooking spray. Fold tortilla over and place in air fryer basket. Spritz top of tortilla with olive oil spray. Lay a butter knife on top of tortilla to keep it folded over. Air fry 5 minutes until cheese is melted and bubbly.

4 Remove quesadilla from air fryer, cut into thirds, and serve.

PER SERVING

CALORIES: 290 | FAT: 20g | SODIUM: 565mg | CARBOHYDRATES: 23g | FIBER: 12g | SUGAR: 4g | PROTEIN: 14g

Egg and Cheese White Pizza

Just because you're eating plant-based doesn't mean you don't need protein! Adding a fried egg makes this pizza creamier and more savory. Naan bread works great as a ready-made individual pizza crust. Feel free to add more vegetables if you'd like, such as mushrooms or spinach.

Hands-On Time: 3 minutes
Cook Time: 6 minutes

Serves 1

- 1 (50-gram) mini garlic naan bread
- 1 tablespoon olive oil
- 1 large egg
- 2 cherry tomatoes, thinly sliced
- ¼ cup shredded mozzarella cheese
- ¹⁄₁₆ teaspoon coarse sea salt

MINI VEGETABLES

When cooking for one, using mini versions of full-sized vegetables really comes in handy. Cherry tomatoes, petite potatoes, and mini sweet peppers are all great examples of vegetables that are appropriate for a single-serving size. You won't have a half-used bell pepper that hides in the back of your refrigerator ever again.

1. On a cutting board, lay out naan. Baste with oil.

2. Place naan in air fryer basket. You may need to adjust naan in the air fryer so egg stays on naan, or place naan on an oven-safe plate with edges that round up.

3. Crack egg into center of naan. Top with tomatoes, mozzarella, and salt. Air fry at 375°F for 6 minutes.

4. Remove from air fryer and serve.

PER SERVING

CALORIES: 411 | **FAT:** 25g | **SODIUM:** 728mg | **CARBOHYDRATES:** 28g | **FIBER:** 1g | **SUGAR:** 4g | **PROTEIN:** 17g

Grilled Cheese Salad

This Grilled Cheese Salad is such a fun twist on a salad. Swap out croutons for bite-sized pieces of a grilled cheese sandwich. Serving on top of a veggie-filled salad finished with ranch dressing makes it a meal.

Hands-On Time: 10 minutes
Cook Time: 5 minutes

Serves 1

1 tablespoon salted butter, softened
1 (¾"-thick) slice white bread
1 (1-ounce) slice American cheese
½ head romaine lettuce, diced
1 medium Roma tomato, diced
1 medium salad cucumber, diced
2 slices red onion, diced
2 baby carrots, grated
2 mini sweet peppers, diced
3 button mushrooms, sliced
2 tablespoons ranch dressing

1 Butter one side of bread. Cut bread in half. Cut cheese slice in half and stack in bread to make a sandwich with buttered side of bread facing out. Secure sandwich with two toothpicks.

2 Place sandwich in air fryer basket and air fry at 350°F for 3 minutes.

3 Open air fryer and discard toothpicks. Flip sandwich and air fry 2 minutes more.

4 Layer all remaining ingredients in a salad bowl.

5 Remove sandwich from air fryer, cut into bite-sized pieces, and top salad with grilled cheese croutons.

PER SERVING

CALORIES: 554 | FAT: 29g | SODIUM: 984mg | CARBOHYDRATES: 58g | FIBER: 13g | SUGAR: 23g | PROTEIN: 18g

Shakshuka

Shakshuka is a meal popular in North African and Middle Eastern countries made of poached eggs in a tomato sauce with onions, garlic, and spices. This is made simple in your air fryer by using a baking dish and a premade marinara sauce. Add a few ingredients to your marinara for a delicious semi-homemade sauce. Serve this over egg noodles to make it more filling.

Hands-On Time: 10 minutes
Cook Time: 11 minutes

Serves 1

1 tablespoon olive oil
2 (½"-thick) slices yellow onion, diced
1 mini sweet pepper, diced
½ teaspoon minced garlic
¼ teaspoon cumin
¼ teaspoon paprika
½ cup jarred marinara sauce
1 large egg
1⁄16 teaspoon coarse sea salt
1⁄16 teaspoon ground black pepper
1 cup egg noodles, cooked
1 teaspoon chopped fresh cilantro

1 In a small baking dish, combine oil, onion, sweet pepper, garlic, cumin, and paprika. Toss lightly to coat. Place dish in air fryer and air fry at 370°F for 4 minutes.

2 Open air fryer and, using pot holders, remove dish. Pour marinara into dish and stir to combine with onion mixture.

3 Crack egg on top of marinara. Sprinkle with salt and black pepper. Return dish to air fryer and air fry at 350°F for 7 minutes.

4 Open air fryer and, using pot holders, remove dish. Serve shakshuka over egg noodles, sprinkled with cilantro.

PER SERVING

CALORIES: 517 | **FAT:** 22g | **SODIUM:** 1,012mg | **CARBOHYDRATES:** 60g | **FIBER:** 6g | **SUGAR:** 12g | **PROTEIN:** 17g

Teriyaki Tofu and Broccoli Stir-Fry

Stir-fry in the air fryer is simple and delicious! Tofu is the featured ingredient in this dish—not only does it add protein, but it takes on the flavor of the sauce. Use your favorite vegetables, like peppers, mushrooms, and broccoli, as well as a cup of ready-to-serve rice for a complete meal.

Hands-On Time: 10 minutes
Cook Time: 14 minutes

Serves 1

- **7 ounces extra-firm tofu**
- **1 mini sweet pepper, cut into ½" chunks**
- **2 button mushrooms, sliced**
- **½ cup broccoli florets, chopped**
- **½ cup teriyaki sauce**
- **1 (4-ounce) cup pineapple tidbits**
- **4 ounces ready-to-serve brown rice**

SINGLE-SERVING PRODUCTS

Single-serving products are very helpful when cooking for one. Rather than having to open a whole can of pineapple or make just 1 cup of rice, you can find preportioned fruit cups, rice and quinoa cups, and more. This way, you do not make as much food waste.

1 Remove tofu from package and place on a medium paper towel–lined plate. Lay another paper towel on top of tofu. Place a cast iron pan on top of the paper towel. Let tofu sit 15 minutes to extract water.

2 Remove pan and paper towels from tofu. Cut tofu into bite-sized cubes.

3 In a medium bowl, combine tofu, pepper, mushrooms, broccoli, teriyaki sauce, and pineapple cup (with juice). Toss to coat completely. Cover bowl and marinate in refrigerator 20 minutes.

4 Spray tray in air fryer basket with nonstick cooking spray. Remove bowl from refrigerator and spread tofu and vegetables in air fryer basket. Air fry at 400°F for 7 minutes. Open air fryer and shake to toss contents. Air fry 7 minutes more.

5 While stir-fry is cooking, heat rice in microwave. Pour rice onto large plate. Top with tofu and vegetables from air fryer and serve.

PER SERVING

CALORIES: 583 | **FAT:** 13g | **SODIUM:** 5,545mg | **CARBOHYDRATES:** 83g | **FIBER:** 7g | **SUGAR:** 40g | **PROTEIN:** 35g

Zucchini Boats

Zucchini is one of the most versatile vegetables. It really takes on whatever flavors you add. It's also a great vessel for dinner when filled with peppers, tomatoes, onion, mozzarella, and orzo. This recipe has an Italian spin, but you could easily substitute taco seasoning for the basil and oregano for more of a Mexican flair.

Hands-On Time: 15 minutes
Cook Time: 9 minutes

Serves 1

- 1 medium zucchini
- 2 (½"-thick) slices yellow onion, diced
- 1 mini sweet pepper, diced
- 2 cherry tomatoes, diced
- 2 (1-ounce) slices fresh mozzarella
- 1 teaspoon olive oil
- ½ teaspoon minced garlic
- ¼ teaspoon dried oregano
- ¼ teaspoon dried basil
- 1⁄16 teaspoon coarse sea salt
- 1⁄16 teaspoon ground black pepper
- ¼ cup cooked orzo

SWAPS FOR ORZO

Orzo is a rice-shaped pasta, and it's a great option for salads or stuffed vegetables. If you don't have orzo, you can easily use any type of rice or quinoa instead.

1 Slice zucchini in half lengthwise. Using a spoon, scoop out seeds and middle of zucchini to make boat for filling.

2 In a medium bowl, mix onion, mini sweet pepper, tomatoes, mozzarella, oil, garlic, oregano, basil, salt, black pepper, and orzo.

3 Spoon vegetable and orzo mixture into boats. Place zucchini boats in air fryer. Air fry at 370°F for 9 minutes.

4 Remove boats from air fryer and serve.

PER SERVING

CALORIES: 314 | FAT: 13g | SODIUM: 240mg | CARBOHYDRATES: 34g | FIBER: 5g | SUGAR: 13g | PROTEIN: 15g

Portobello Fajitas

Looking for a delicious plant-based yet meaty meal? These fajitas might surprise you with how flavorful they are. Meaty portobello mushrooms combined with peppers, onions, and fajita seasoning come together for your very own fajita night. Bring out the toppings too—sour cream, cheese, salsa, and more!

Hands-On Time: 5 minutes
Cook Time: 11 minutes

Serves 1

- 1 medium portobello mushroom, stemmed and thinly sliced
- 2 mini sweet peppers, thinly sliced
- 2 (½"-thick) slices yellow onion, cut into thin strips
- 1 tablespoon Tajín Clásico Seasoning
- 1 teaspoon olive oil
- 2 (6") low-carb flour tortillas
- ¼ cup freshly grated Colby jack cheese
- 2 tablespoons salsa
- 2 tablespoons sour cream

1 In a medium bowl, combine mushroom, peppers, onion, Tajín seasoning, and oil. Toss to coat.

2 Place vegetables in air fryer basket. Air fry at 380°F for 5 minutes.

3 Open air fryer and, using tongs, toss vegetables. Air fry 5 minutes more.

4 Open air fryer and remove vegetables from air fryer basket.

5 Lay tortillas in air fryer. Keep tortillas flat by laying two butter knives across them. Air fry at 360°F for 1 minute to warm.

6 Open air fryer and transfer tortillas to a large plate. Top tortillas with vegetables, Colby jack, salsa, and sour cream. Serve.

PER SERVING

CALORIES: 408 | FAT: 22g | SODIUM: 3,201mg | CARBOHYDRATES: 47g | FIBER: 22g | SUGAR: 11g | PROTEIN: 20g

Stuffed Butternut Squash

This delicious, healthy Stuffed Butternut Squash is filled with quinoa, cranberries, kale, and chickpeas. It's an easy, satisfying vegetarian dish that's perfect for fall! This balanced dish has sweetness from the squash and cranberries, saltiness from the feta, and crunch from the kale.

Hands-On Time: 10 minutes
Cook Time: 30 minutes

Serves 1

½ medium butternut squash
2 teaspoons olive oil, divided
⅟₁₆ teaspoon coarse sea salt
⅟₁₆ teaspoon ground black pepper
1 kale leaf
¼ cup cooked quinoa
¼ cup drained chickpeas
2 tablespoons dried cranberries, chopped
2 tablespoons crumbled feta cheese
1 teaspoon lemon juice
½ teaspoon minced garlic
¼ teaspoon Italian seasoning

AQUAFABA

The liquid from chickpeas, beans, and tofu is very useful. It's called aquafaba. It can be substituted for egg whites in many recipes. Save it in an airtight container for a week in the refrigerator, or freeze for up to 3 months.

1 Scoop seeds out of squash and score squash with a paring knife. Drizzle with 1 teaspoon oil and season with salt and pepper.

2 Place squash in air fryer basket. Air fry at 380°F for 25 minutes.

3 In a medium bowl, tear kale into bite-sized pieces. Add quinoa, chickpeas, cranberries, feta, lemon juice, remaining 1 teaspoon oil, garlic, and Italian seasoning and stir.

4 Open air fryer basket and, using tongs, remove squash.

5 Once squash is cool enough to handle, scoop out flesh, leaving ¾" border around edges and bottom. Spoon filling into squash.

6 Return squash to air fryer basket and air fry at 360°F for 5 minutes.

7 Remove squash from air fryer with a large spatula. Serve.

PER SERVING

CALORIES: 379 | FAT: 14g | SODIUM: 383mg | CARBOHYDRATES: 58g | FIBER: 9g | SUGAR: 17g | PROTEIN: 10g

Mushroom Burger

The normal go-to for a veggie burger is a black bean burger, but it's not convenient to make when cooking for one. Mushrooms are a great alternative that make a delicious vegetarian burger that can be done in your air fryer.

Hands-On Time: 10 minutes
Cook Time: 10 minutes

Serves 1

- **4 button mushrooms, stemmed**
- **1 large egg**
- **3 tablespoons shredded Cheddar cheese**
- **2 tablespoons bread crumbs**
- **2 tablespoons diced white onion**
- **2 tablespoons all-purpose flour**
- **⅛ teaspoon salt**
- **⅛ teaspoon minced garlic**
- **¹⁄₁₆ teaspoon ground black pepper**
- **1 hamburger bun**

1 Grate mushrooms with the large holes of a cheese grater.

2 In a medium bowl, combine mushrooms, egg, Cheddar, bread crumbs, onion, flour, salt, garlic, and pepper. Form mixture into a patty. Lay patty on a sheet of parchment paper that fits into your air fryer.

3 Place parchment with patty in air fryer basket and air fry at 360°F for 5 minutes.

4 Open air fryer and, using a thin metal spatula, flip patty. Air fry 5 minutes more.

5 Open air fryer and remove burger. Serve on bun.

PER SERVING

CALORIES: 405 | FAT: 13g | SODIUM: 808mg | CARBOHYDRATES: 48g | FIBER: 3g | SUGAR: 6g | PROTEIN: 21g

Kale, Mushroom, and Tomato Strata

Strata is a fancy name for a layered casserole. It's delicious and often served for brunch. Eggs, bread, and vegetables a l combine for a comforting, savory bread pudding casserole.

Hands-On Time: 5 minutes
Cook Time: 15 minutes

Serves 1

4 button mushrooms, sliced
4 cherry tomatoes, sliced
1 kale leaf, torn into bite-sized pieces
1 teaspoon olive oil
½ teaspoon dried rosemary
2 (¾"-thick) slices white bread, diced
¼ cup shredded Swiss cheese
2 large eggs
¼ cup heavy cream
¼ teaspoon Dijon mustard
⅟₁₆ teaspoon coarse sea salt
⅟₁₆ teaspoon ground black pepper

1 Spray a small baking dish with nonstick cooking spray. Add mushrooms, tomatoes, kale, oil, and rosemary to dish and toss to combine.

2 Place bread cubes in one half of air fryer basket. Place dish with vegetables in other half of basket. Air fry at 400°F for 5 minutes. This will dry out the bread cubes just a bit.

3 Open air fryer and, using pot holders, remove dish and bread cubes. Add bread cubes and cheese to dish with vegetables.

4 In a medium bowl, beat eggs, cream, mustard, salt, and pepper. Pour egg mixture into dish with bread and vegetables. Push bread cubes into egg mixture. Cover and refrigerate 10 minutes.

5 Remove dish from refrigerator and uncover. Place dish in air fryer and air fry at 320°F for 10 minutes until bread cubes are golden brown.

6 Using pot holders, remove dish from air fryer. Let cool 10 minutes. Serve warm.

PER SERVING

CALORIES: 706 | FAT: 43g | SODIUM: 683mg | CARBOHYDRATES: 44g | FIBER: 4g | SUGAR: 10g | PROTEIN: 30g

Roasted Cauliflower Jerk Tacos

Roasted cauliflower is a delicious alternative to meat in tacos. Cauliflower takes on the flavor of whatever seasoning you add to it. The spicy seasonings in this recipe are quickly cooled by the avocado and sour cream. If you're not a fan of jerk seasoning, you can use fajita or Cajun seasoning instead.

Hands-On Time: 3 minutes
Cook Time: 10 minutes

Serves 1

1 cup bite-sized cauliflower
  florets
1 tablespoon olive oil
1 teaspoon jerk seasoning
3 (5") corn tortillas
½ medium ripe avocado,
  pitted, peeled, and sliced
3 cherry tomatoes, sliced
3 teaspoons sour cream
1 teaspoon chopped fresh
  cilantro
Juice of ½ medium lime

1 In a medium bowl, toss cauliflower, oil, and jerk seasoning.

2 Place cauliflower in air fryer basket and air fry at 360°F for 8 minutes.

3 When cauliflower is fork-tender, lay tortillas on top of cauliflower in air fryer. Air fry 2 minutes more.

4 Remove tortillas and lay on a large plate. Top with cauliflower, avocado, and tomatoes. Then top with sour cream, cilantro, and lime juice.

PER SERVING

CALORIES: 455 | **FAT:** 27g | **SODIUM:** 222mg | **CARBOHYDRATES:** 47g | **FIBER:** 12g | **SUGAR:** 5g | **PROTEIN:** 8g

Italian Stuffed Peppers

Stuffed peppers are such a delicious dish and have all the heartiness you need in a filling meal. Plus, they're surprisingly easy to make for one in your air fryer. These stuffed peppers reheat very well, so you can double the recipe and have lunch made for the next day. Use any color pepper you like, but the orange and yellow are sweeter than the green variety.

Hands-On Time: 10 minutes
Cook Time: 10 minutes

Serves 1

- 1 medium orange bell pepper
- 1 (2-ounce) slice extra-firm tofu
- 2 cherry tomatoes, diced
- 2 button mushrooms, diced
- ½ leaf kale, diced
- ¼ cup cooked orzo
- 3 tablespoons jarred spaghetti sauce
- ⅟₁₆ teaspoon coarse sea salt
- 1 tablespoon shredded mozzarella cheese

COOK-AHEAD PASTA AND RICE

If you have a recipe that calls for ¼ cup of cooked rice or pasta, make a larger batch of 1–2 cups during the weekend. Then, during the week, meal prep is quicker because your grains are already cooked. Store them in an airtight container in your refrigerator.

1. Slice top off pepper and discard. Using a spoon, scoop out any ribs and seeds from inside of pepper. Slice pepper in half to make two "boats."

2. Remove tofu from package and place tofu slice on a medium paper towel–lined plate. Lay another paper towel on top of tofu. Place a cast iron pan on top of the paper towel. Let tofu sit 15 minutes to extract water.

3. Remove pan and paper towels from tofu. Grate tofu with the large holes of a cheese grater. In a medium bowl, combine tofu, tomatoes, mushrooms, kale, orzo, spaghetti sauce, and salt. Toss to combine. Spoon tofu mixture into pepper halves.

4. Spray air fryer tray with nonstick cooking spray. Place stuffed pepper halves in air fryer. Air fry at 350°F for 5 minutes. Open air fryer and add mozzarella to tops of pepper halves. Air fry 5 minutes more.

5. Remove stuffed peppers from air fryer and serve.

PER SERVING

CALORIES: 220 | **FAT:** 5g | **SODIUM:** 374mg | **CARBOHYDRATES:** 31g | **FIBER:** 6g | **SUGAR:** 11g | **PROTEIN:** 13g

Zucchini Lasagna Roll-Ups

Lasagna roll-ups are delicious. Plus, they are even healthier when made with zucchini instead of pasta! Stuffing these roll-ups with ricotta, mozzarella, mushrooms, spinach, and marinara sauce makes them filling too.

Hands-On Time: 15 minutes
Cook Time: 13 minutes

Serves 1

- 1 large zucchini, halved lengthwise
- 3 tablespoons ricotta cheese
- 3 tablespoons shredded mozzarella cheese
- 1 large egg white
- ½ teaspoon Italian seasoning
- ½ cup jarred marinara sauce
- 2 button mushrooms, sliced
- 6 spinach leaves
- 1 tablespoon grated vegetarian Parmesan cheese
- 1 tablespoon bread crumbs
- 1 teaspoon unsalted butter, melted

1 Using a mandoline, slice 3 long strips (¾"-thick) from center of 1 zucchini half for "noodles." Set remaining zucchini half aside for another use.

2 In a medium bowl, mix ricotta, mozzarella, egg white, and Italian seasoning.

3 Spray a small baking dish with nonstick cooking spray. Pour marinara into dish.

4 On a cutting board, lay out zucchini noodles. Spread ricotta mixture on noodles. Lay mushrooms and spinach on top of ricotta mixture, keeping vegetables toward center of noodles. Tightly roll zucchini noodles into roll-ups.

5 Place roll-ups seam-side down in dish with marinara. Place dish in air fryer and air fry at 350°F for 10 minutes.

6 While zucchini roll-ups are cooking, mix Parmesan, bread crumbs, and butter.

7 Open air fryer and sprinkle bread crumb mixture on top of roll-ups. Air fry 3 minutes more.

8 Using pot holders, remove dish from air fryer. Let roll-ups cool slightly before serving.

PER SERVING

CALORIES: 337 | FAT: 15g | SODIUM: 954mg | CARBOHYDRATES: 27g | FIBER: 6g | SUGAR: 13g | PROTEIN: 22g

Tandoori Potato Skewers

This yogurt-based tandoori marinade is full of spices and a has tangy kick from yogurt and lime. Potatoes add a heartiness to these vegetarian skewers, and briefly parcooking the potatoes saves time.

Hands-On Time: 10 minutes
Cook Time: 12 minutes

Serves 1

- 3 petite golden potatoes, diced
- 6 cherry tomatoes
- 6 button mushrooms, stemmed
- 2 mini sweet peppers, diced
- ½ cup nonfat plain Greek yogurt
- 2 teaspoons lime juice
- 1 teaspoon minced garlic
- ½ teaspoon grated fresh ginger
- ½ teaspoon ground cumin
- ½ teaspoon ground coriander
- ½ teaspoon coarse sea salt
- ½ teaspoon garam masala
- ⅟₁₆ teaspoon red pepper flakes

1 Lay potatoes on a wet paper towel and roll up. Microwave potatoes 2 minutes.

2 On four small wooden skewers, alternate potatoes, tomatoes, mushrooms, and sweet peppers.

3 In a small bowl, mix yogurt, lime juice, garlic, ginger, cumin, coriander, salt, garam masala, and red pepper flakes.

4 On a cutting board, heavily baste skewers on all sides with yogurt mixture. Cover with plastic wrap and marinate in refrigerator 30 minutes.

5 Place skewers in air fryer and air fry at 360°F for 5 minutes.

6 Open air fryer and flip skewers. Air fry 5 minutes more.

7 Remove skewers from air fryer and serve with any remaining sauce.

PER SERVING

CALORIES: 261 | **FAT:** 1g | **SODIUM:** 1,028mg | **CARBOHYDRATES:** 48g | **FIBER:** 7g | **SUGAR:** 12g | **PROTEIN:** 20g

Crunchy Tofu Nuggets

These Crunchy Tofu Nuggets will make you feel like a kid again. Serve them up with French fries and an easy honey mustard dipping sauce for a quick dinner any night of the week.

Hands-On Time: 10 minutes
Cook Time: 10 minutes

Serves 1

7 ounces extra-firm tofu
⅓ cup all-purpose flour
1 teaspoon coarse sea salt
1 large egg
1 tablespoon water
½ cup panko bread crumbs
1 tablespoon mayonnaise
1 tablespoon honey mustard

TOFU PRESS

If you are a frequent user of tofu, you might want to invest in a tofu press. In most cases, it's a plastic box that presses down on the tofu. The liquid drains out underneath the block of tofu. Pressing the liquid out of tofu is essential to making sure your bites are as crispy as possible.

1 Remove tofu from package and place on a medium paper towel–lined plate. Lay another paper towel on top of tofu. Place a cast iron pan on top of the paper towel. Let tofu sit 15 minutes to extract water. Remove pan and paper towels from tofu. Cut tofu into six 2" cubes.

2 Prepare breading station with three medium dishes. Mix flour and salt in the first dish. Beat egg and water in the second dish. Spread panko in the third dish.

3 Dredge tofu in flour, coating all sides. Dip tofu in egg, making sure to coat completely. Lastly, dredge tofu in panko, pressing panko onto all sides.

4 Place tofu nuggets in air fryer basket with about 1" of space between. Spritz one side with olive oil spray. Air fry at 380°F for 5 minutes.

5 Open air fryer, flip nuggets, and spritz again with olive oil spray. Air fry 5 minutes more.

6 While nuggets are cooking, mix mayonnaise and honey mustard in a small bowl.

7 Using tongs, remove nuggets from air fryer. Serve with sauce.

PER SERVING

CALORIES: 492 | **FAT:** 29g | **SODIUM:** 1,220mg | **CARBOHYDRATES:** 29g | **FIBER:** 3g | **SUGAR:** 4g | **PROTEIN:** 26g

Crispy Buffalo Tofu Salad

Looking for a healthy salad with a bit of a kick? This Crispy Buffalo Tofu Salad is light and cool to balance the buffalo sauce. Diced celery and ranch dressing add the crunch and creaminess for a perfect meal.

Hands-On Time: 10 minutes
Cook Time: 9 minutes

Serves 1

- 3 ounces extra-firm tofu
- 2 cups romaine lettuce, torn into bite-sized pieces
- 4 cherry tomatoes, sliced
- ½ medium stalk celery, diced
- 1 tablespoon pickled jalapeño slices
- ¼ cup shredded Colby jack cheese
- 2 ounces nacho-flavored chips
- ¼ cup buffalo sauce
- 2 tablespoons ranch dressing

1 Remove tofu from package and place on a medium paper towel–lined plate. Lay another paper towel on top of tofu. Place a cast iron pan on top of the paper towel. Let tofu sit 15 minutes to extract water. Remove pan and paper towels from tofu. Cut tofu into bite-sized cubes.

2 Place tofu in air fryer and air fry at 370°F for 5 minutes.

3 Open air fryer and flip tofu cubes. Air fry 4 minutes more.

4 While tofu is cooking, prepare salad. Place romaine in a medium bowl. Add tomatoes, celery, jalapeño, and Colby jack. Slightly break up chips into smaller pieces and spread on top of salad.

5 Remove tofu from air fryer and toss in buffalo sauce. Add tofu to salad.

6 Top salad with ranch dressing and serve.

PER SERVING

CALORIES: 645 | **FAT:** 40g | **SODIUM:** 2,808mg | **CARBOHYDRATES:** 46g | **FIBER:** 7g | **SUGAR:** 7g | **PROTEIN:** 22g

Greek Stuffed Tomatoes

This stuffed tomato recipe pays homage to Greek flavors with feta cheese, oregano, and kalamata olives. Using the entire tomato adds extra flavor and filling to your stuffed tomatoes. Serve these tomatoes with a slice of crusty bread, or with a hearty whole grain like couscous or quinoa, for a delicious meal.

Hands-On Time: 10 minutes
Cook Time: 10 minutes

Serves 1

2 medium Campari tomatoes
1⁄16 teaspoon salt
1⁄4 cup crumbled feta cheese
6 kalamata olives, diced
2 tablespoons grated vegetarian Parmesan cheese
1 tablespoon panko bread crumbs
1 teaspoon dried oregano
1 teaspoon salted butter, melted
1⁄4 teaspoon garlic salt

1 Core tomatoes and cut 2" circle at top of each tomato. Scoop tomato pulp into a medium bowl.

2 Sprinkle insides of tomato shells with salt and place upside down on a paper towel. Let tomatoes drain while you make filling.

3 Add feta, olives, Parmesan, panko, oregano, butter, and garlic salt to bowl with tomato pulp. Spoon feta mixture into tomato shells.

4 Place stuffed tomatoes in air fryer. Air fry at 350°F for 10 minutes.

5 Using tongs, remove stuffed tomatoes from air fryer and serve.

PER SERVING

CALORIES: 303 | **FAT:** 21g | **SODIUM:** 1,596mg | **CARBOHYDRATES:** 18g | **FIBER:** 3g | **SUGAR:** 8g | **PROTEIN:** 11g

Parmesan and Herb–Crusted Tofu

Parmesan and Herb–Crusted Tofu is a great addition to pasta any night of the week! Topping your tofu with a creamy Parmesan crust gives you a crunchy, cheesy entrée. Serve on top of pasta and sauce or with a salad.

Hands-On Time: 5 minutes
Cook Time: 8 minutes

Serves 1

- **7 ounces extra-firm tofu**
- **2 teaspoons mayonnaise**
- **2 tablespoons grated vegetarian Parmesan cheese**
- **2 tablespoons panko bread crumbs**
- **1 teaspoon minced garlic**
- **½ teaspoon Italian seasoning**
- **⅛ teaspoon red pepper flakes**
- **¹⁄₁₆ teaspoon coarse sea salt**

1 Remove tofu from package and place on a medium paper towel–lined plate. Lay another paper towel on top of tofu. Place a cast iron pan on top of the paper towel. Let tofu sit 15 minutes to extract water. Remove pan and paper towels from tofu. Cut tofu into 2 slices.

2 Place tofu slices in air fryer basket. Air fry at 380°F for 4 minutes.

3 In a small bowl, mix mayonnaise, Parmesan, panko, garlic, Italian seasoning, red pepper flakes, and salt.

4 Open air fryer and flip tofu. Top with Parmesan mixture and lightly press into tofu. Lower temperature to 350°F and air fry 4 minutes more.

5 Using a spatula, remove tofu from air fryer and serve.

PER SERVING

CALORIES: 327 | **FAT:** 19g | **SODIUM:** 287mg | **CARBOHYDRATES:** 17g | **FIBER:** 3g | **SUGAR:** 1g | **PROTEIN:** 23g

Mexican Stuffed Sweet Potatoes

Sweet potatoes are delicious and very nutritious. This recipe takes your favorite Mexican toppings and brings a baked sweet potato to a new level. Combine mini sweet peppers, corn, tomatoes, and a frozen black bean patty for the stuffing. Then top with lime, cilantro, and a quick avocado cream sauce for a filling dinner.

Hands-On Time: 10 minutes
Cook Time: 25 minutes

Serves 1

- 1 small sweet potato, scrubbed clean
- 1 teaspoon olive oil
- ⅟₁₆ teaspoon coarse sea salt
- 1 mini sweet pepper, diced
- 1 (1"-thick) slice red onion, diced
- 3 cherry tomatoes, diced
- ¼ cup frozen corn
- 1 teaspoon Tajín Clásico Seasoning
- 1 (2½-ounce) frozen black bean burger
- ½ medium ripe avocado, pitted and peeled
- 2 tablespoons sour cream
- 1 medium lime, halved
- 1 tablespoon chopped fresh cilantro

1   Pierce potato with paring knife 3–4 times. Rub outside of potato with oil and salt. Place potato in air fryer basket. Air fry at 380°F for 15 minutes.

2   Combine pepper, onion, tomatoes, corn, and Tajín seasoning in a small oven-safe baking dish. Spritz with olive oil spray and toss.

3   After 15 minutes are up, open air fryer and place dish and black bean patty in air fryer with potato. Lower temperature to 370°F and air fry 10 minutes more.

4   Meanwhile, in a medium bowl, mash avocado with sour cream and juice from 1 lime half.

5   Check potato for doneness—a paring knife should slide in easily and potato should be soft in center. If needed, air fry 3–5 minutes more. Using tongs and a pot holder, carefully remove potato, black bean patty, and baking dish from air fryer. Break up patty and mix with peppers.

6   On a medium plate, slice potato lengthwise and fill with pepper mixture. Top with avocado cream sauce and cilantro. Squeeze remaining lime half over potato and serve.

PER SERVING

CALORIES: 495 | **FAT:** 21g | **SODIUM:** 1,344mg | **CARBOHYDRATES:** 68g | **FIBER:** 16g | **SUGAR:** 17g | **PROTEIN:** 12g

Sweet Potato Brussels Sprout Hash

This vegetarian sweet potato hash is delicious and wholesome! With sweet potato, Brussels sprouts, peppers, mushrooms, and tomatoes, it's a great meal any time of day. The protein from the egg rounds out this healthier meal option.

Hands-On Time: 5 minutes
Cook Time: 15 minutes

Serves 1

- 1 small sweet potato, peeled and cut into ½" cubes
- 6 Brussels sprouts, quartered
- 2 tablespoons olive oil, divided
- ¼ teaspoon coarse sea salt, divided
- ¼ teaspoon ground black pepper, divided
- 1 mini sweet pepper, cut into ½" pieces
- 4 button mushrooms, cut into ½" pieces
- 6 cherry tomatoes, cut into ½" pieces
- 1 large egg
- ⅛ teaspoon hot sauce

1. In a medium bowl, toss potato and Brussels sprouts with 1 tablespoon oil, ¹⁄₁₆ teaspoon salt, and ¹⁄₁₆ teaspoon black pepper. Place potato and Brussels sprouts in air fryer basket. Air fry at 380°F for 10 minutes.

2. In a separate medium bowl, combine mini sweet pepper, mushrooms, tomatoes, remaining 1 tablespoon oil, ⅛ teaspoon salt, and ⅛ teaspoon black pepper. Toss to coat.

3. Open air fryer and, using tongs, toss potato and Brussels sprouts. Add remaining vegetables to air fryer.

4. Spray a ramekin with nonstick cooking spray. Crack egg into ramekin and sprinkle with remaining ¹⁄₁₆ teaspoon each salt and black pepper. Push vegetables in air fryer basket to the side to make room for ramekin, then place ramekin in air fryer basket. Lower temperature to 360°F and air fry 5 minutes more.

5. Remove potato mixture from air fryer and place on a large plate. With pot holders, remove ramekin. Using a spatula, loosen egg from ramekin and place on top of hash. Serve hash with hot sauce.

PER SERVING

CALORIES: 454 | **FAT:** 31g | **SODIUM:** 627mg | **CARBOHYDRATES:** 31g | **FIBER:** 9g | **SUGAR:** 12g | **PROTEIN:** 15g

Roasted Cauliflower Steak with Chimichurri Sauce

Cauliflower steak is a great way to enjoy this extremely healthy vegetable. Roasting in your air fryer with salt, pepper, and olive oil brings out all the flavor in your steak. Top it with a made-from-scratch chimichurri sauce for a delicious main dish.

Hands-On Time: 3 minutes
Cook Time: 12 minutes

Serves 1

- 1 (1½"-thick) slice cauliflower
- ¼ teaspoon coarse sea salt, divided
- ⅛ teaspoon ground black pepper, divided
- ¼ cup fresh cilantro
- 2 tablespoons fresh Italian parsley
- ½ teaspoon dried oregano
- ½ teaspoon minced garlic
- 3 tablespoons olive oil
- Juice of ½ medium lime
- 1 teaspoon red wine vinegar
- ⅛ teaspoon red pepper flakes

1 Lay cauliflower steak in air fryer basket. Spritz with olive oil spray and sprinkle with ⅟₁₆ teaspoon each salt and pepper. Air fry at 400°F for 6 minutes.

2 Open air fryer and flip steak. Spritz again with olive oil spray and sprinkle with ⅟₁₆ teaspoon salt and remaining ⅟₁₆ teaspoon pepper. Air fry 6 minutes more.

3 While steak is cooking, combine all remaining ingredients, including remaining ⅛ teaspoon salt, in a mini food processor or blender. Pulse until smooth to make chimichurri sauce.

4 Remove steak from air fryer, pour chimichurri sauce over steak, and serve.

PER SERVING

CALORIES: 400 | **FAT:** 40g | **SODIUM:** 529mg | **CARBOHYDRATES:** 10g | **FIBER:** 4g | **SUGAR:** 3g | **PROTEIN:** 3g

Desserts

Up until this point, the savory, spicy, salty, umami dishes have been the stars of the air fryer. No longer! This chapter is filled with fruity, fried, creamy, sweet desserts. There is something that will appeal to you whether you're a chocolate lover or a fruit lover or you're looking to try something new. This chapter will make you feel like you have a live-in pastry chef.

This chapter features a lot of fruit-fueled recipes like Grilled Pineapple, Eggless Banana Bread, Blueberry Cobbler, and a lot more. For those who are looking to recreate old favorites, there's the Peanut Butter Cookies, Blueberry Muffins, or Chocolate Melting Cake. If you're looking to try something totally new, try the Chocolate Chip Doughnut Bread Pudding, Chocolate Hazelnut and Strawberry Fluffadilla, or Strawberry Cheesecake Wrap. Whatever you choose, it will be delicious. Let's get air frying!

Fried Sandwich Cookies

These air fryer Fried Sandwich Cookies are delicious like the fair food but without all the grease. These fried cookies are dipped in a light batter and then air fried until the batter is golden brown and the inside is melty. You may use Bisquick as your baking mix.

Hands-On Time: 10 minutes
Cook Time: 6 minutes

Serves 1

1 large egg, beaten
¼ cup baking mix
1 tablespoon 2% milk
½ teaspoon vanilla extract
3 overstuffed chocolate
    sandwich cookies
1 teaspoon confectioners'
    sugar

1. Line air fryer basket with parchment paper and lightly spray with nonstick cooking spray.

2. Spoon half of egg into a small bowl, discarding the rest. Add baking mix, milk, and vanilla.

3. Dip cookies into batter, letting excess drip into bowl.

4. Place cookies on corners of parchment in air fryer in a single layer, making sure they are not touching. Placing on corners will prevent parchment from blowing and covering cookies. Air fry at 350°F for 6 minutes.

5. Remove cookies from air fryer and trim edges. Dust with sugar before serving.

PER SERVING

CALORIES: 425 | **FAT:** 19g | **SODIUM:** 521mg | **CARBOHYDRATES:** 55g | **FIBER:** 1g | **SUGAR:** 23g | **PROTEIN:** 9g

Roasted Honey Pears

Pears are naturally sweet, but once they're air fried with a touch of honey, you'll be amazed at how they melt in your mouth. These are also delicious with a scoop of butter pecan ice cream.

Hands-On Time: 5 minutes
Cook Time: 5 minutes

Serves 1

1 small Bartlett pear
2 teaspoons salted butter
2 teaspoons honey
1/16 teaspoon ground cinnamon
1 tablespoon chopped walnuts

1 Cut pear in half and, using a spoon or melon baller, scoop out core. Score pear with a paring knife in a crosshatch pattern. Place 1 teaspoon butter in each scooped-out core. Drizzle with honey and sprinkle with cinnamon.

2 Place pear halves in air fryer basket. Air fry at 350°F for 5 minutes.

3 Remove pear halves from air fryer and place on a small plate. Top with walnuts and serve.

PER SERVING

CALORIES: 269 | **FAT:** 12g | **SODIUM:** 61mg | **CARBOHYDRATES:** 39g | **FIBER:** 6g | **SUGAR:** 29g | **PROTEIN:** 2g

Grilled Pineapple

This air fryer Grilled Pineapple is fun to cook and an amazingly simple dessert that anybody can make in just a very short time. These are great served with some vanilla ice cream.

Hands-On Time: 10 minutes
Cook Time: 10 minutes

Serves 1

2 tablespoons light brown sugar
½ teaspoon ground cinnamon
4 pineapple spears
1 tablespoon salted butter, melted

1 In a small bowl, mix sugar and cinnamon.

2 Lay pineapple spears on a rimmed baking sheet and pour butter over spears, coating all sides. Remove spears from butter and roll in sugar mixture until coated.

3 Place pineapple in a single layer in air fryer. Air fry at 400°F for 5 minutes.

4 Mix remaining butter with remaining sugar mixture. Open air fryer, flip pineapple, and brush with butter mixture. Air fry 5 minutes more.

5 Remove from air fryer and serve.

PER SERVING

CALORIES: 358 | **FAT:** 11g | **SODIUM:** 101mg | **CARBOHYDRATES:** 68g | **FIBER:** 5g | **SUGAR:** 57g | **PROTEIN:** 2g

Peanut Butter Cookies

These air fryer Peanut Butter Cookies are like your favorite childhood cookie but cooked even faster! These cookies have double the peanut butter and are sprinkled with sugar. They will be the perfect sweet treat any day of the week.

Hands-On Time: 10 minutes
Cook Time: 7 minutes

Serves 1

- 3 tablespoons all-purpose flour
- ⅛ teaspoon baking soda
- ⅛ teaspoon baking powder
- 1/16 teaspoon salt
- 2 tablespoons peanut butter
- 1½ teaspoons salted butter, softened
- 2 tablespoons light brown sugar
- 1 tablespoon applesauce
- ¼ teaspoon vanilla extract
- ½ teaspoon 2% milk
- 1 tablespoon granulated sugar

1 In a medium bowl, mix flour, baking soda, baking powder, and salt.

2 In a separate medium bowl, using an electric hand mixer on medium speed, beat together peanut butter and butter. Add brown sugar, applesauce, vanilla, and milk. Mix until combined.

3 Slowly add flour mixture and mix until combined, being careful to not overmix.

4 Refrigerate dough for 30 minutes.

5 Lay out a sheet of parchment paper that fits into your air fryer. Using a small cookie scoop, scoop 4 balls of dough onto parchment. Sprinkle cookies with granulated sugar. Using a fork, flatten dough in a cross-hatch pattern.

6 Move parchment to air fryer and air fry at 300°F for 7 minutes.

7 Open air fryer and let cookies rest 1–2 minutes before removing so they have time to set up. Cookies will be soft.

8 Remove parchment from air fryer. Using a spatula, transfer cookies to a large plate. Enjoy.

PER SERVING

CALORIES: 485 | **FAT:** 20g | **SODIUM:** 479mg | **CARBOHYDRATES:** 67g | **FIBER:** 3g | **SUGAR:** 44g | **PROTEIN:** 10g

Eggless Banana Bread

Don't let an egg allergy prevent you from enjoying yummy treats like banana bread. Bananas themselves are a great binder, and you won't even miss the egg. This bread is best when served warm with a pat of butter.

Hands-On Time: 10 minutes
Cook Time: 13 minutes

Serves 1

1½ tablespoons salted butter, softened
3 tablespoons granulated sugar
¼ cup all-purpose flour
⅛ teaspoon baking soda
¼ teaspoon baking powder
¹⁄₁₆ teaspoon salt
1 small banana, mashed

1 In a medium bowl, using an electric hand mixer on medium speed, cream together butter and sugar. Add flour, baking soda, baking powder, and salt and mix until combined, being careful to not overmix.

2 Fold banana into batter.

3 Spray a mini loaf pan with nonstick cooking spray. Pour batter into pan.

4 Cover tightly with aluminum foil. Place loaf pan in air fryer and air fry at 340°F for 8 minutes.

5 Open air fryer basket and remove foil. Air fry 5 minutes more.

6 Using pot holders, remove pan from air fryer and let cool at least 5 minutes.

7 Remove bread from pan and serve warm.

PER SERVING

CALORIES: 499 | **FAT:** 16g | **SODIUM:** 560mg | **CARBOHYDRATES:** 85g | **FIBER:** 3g | **SUGAR:** 50g | **PROTEIN:** 5g

Banana Cake

This air fryer Banana Cake is a light and fluffy, super-moist cake with so much banana flavor! Baking cake in the air fryer is easy as well. This cake is topped with a quick buttercream frosting.

Hands-On Time: 10 minutes
Cook Time: 15 minutes

Serves 1

Banana Cake
½ small banana
⅛ teaspoon lemon juice
2 tablespoons light brown sugar
1 tablespoon salted butter, softened
1 tablespoon 2% milk
1 tablespoon applesauce
¼ teaspoon vanilla extract
¼ cup all-purpose flour
⅛ teaspoon baking soda
⅛ teaspoon baking powder
⅛ teaspoon ground cinnamon
1/16 teaspoon coarse sea salt
1 teaspoon chopped pecans

Frosting
1 tablespoon salted butter, softened
1 ounce full-fat cream cheese, softened
⅛ teaspoon vanilla extract
⅛ teaspoon lemon juice
½ cup confectioners' sugar

1 Spray a ramekin with nonstick cooking spray.

2 To make Banana Cake: In a medium bowl, mash banana and lemon juice. Set aside.

3 In a pint jar, using an electric hand mixer on medium speed, beat together sugar and butter. Add milk, applesauce, and vanilla and mix on high speed until combined. Add flour, baking soda, baking powder, cinnamon, and salt and mix until combined.

4 Spoon batter into bowl with banana mixture and fold together. Pour into ramekin. Sprinkle pecans on top of batter. Place ramekin in air fryer and air fry at 300°F for 15 minutes.

5 To make Frosting: While cake is air frying, in a small bowl, use an electric hand mixer on medium speed to cream together butter and cream cheese until fluffy. Add vanilla and lemon juice and mix until combined. Gradually add sugar and mix until Frosting reaches a thick, spreadable consistency. Cover and refrigerate until use.

6 Using pot holders, remove cake from air fryer and place in freezer 20 minutes. Once cake is cooled, remove from ramekin, frost, and enjoy.

PER SERVING

CALORIES: 789 | FAT: 32g | SODIUM: 637mg | CARBOHYDRATES: 118g | FIBER: 3g | SUGAR: 85g | PROTEIN: 7g

Cookie Cheesecake

Cheesecake is a decadent dessert. Making a mini cheesecake in your air fryer is easy too! Adding chocolate sandwich cookies to the crust and the filling makes for a fun treat in under 30 minutes. This cheesecake isn't overly sweet, but it has a light, creamy texture that you'll love! Serve with some whipped cream for added sweetness.

Hands-On Time: 15 minutes
Cook Time: 12 minutes

Serves 1

Crust
5 chocolate sandwich cookies
1 tablespoon salted butter, melted

Filling
3 ounces full-fat cream cheese, softened
1 tablespoon granulated sugar
2 teaspoons sour cream
¼ teaspoon vanilla extract
1 large egg, beaten

1 To make Crust: Put cookies in a quart-sized plastic zip-top freezer bag. Using a rolling pin, crush cookies. Remove half of cookies that are larger pieces and set aside. In a small bowl, mix 3 tablespoons remaining finely crushed cookie pieces with butter.

2 Spray a ramekin with nonstick cooking spray. Press cookie mixture into bottom of ramekin to make Crust. Place in air fryer and air fry at 350°F for 4 minutes.

3 To make Filling: In a medium mixing bowl, use an electric hand mixer on medium speed to beat cream cheese and sugar until smooth. Add sour cream and vanilla and mix for 30 seconds. Add half of egg to batter and mix, discarding the other half. Using a spatula, fold in reserved larger cookie pieces.

4 Using pot holders, remove ramekin from air fryer and pour batter into ramekin.

5 Return ramekin to air fryer and air fry 8 minutes more.

6 Using pot holders, remove from air fryer and refrigerate at least 3 hours. Serve.

PER SERVING

CALORIES: 809 | **FAT:** 53g | **SODIUM:** 708mg | **CARBOHYDRATES:** 59g | **FIBER:** 2g | **SUGAR:** 40g | **PROTEIN:** 15g

Pineapple Upside-Down Cake

Looking for a fruity classic to try in your air fryer? Try this Pineapple Upside-Down Cake. It's a light vanilla cake with a brown sugar–covered pineapple to top it off. Cake in a ramekin is an easy dessert for one, and you can top it with whipped cream or vanilla ice cream.

Hands-On Time: 10 minutes
Cook Time: 15 minutes

Serves 1

2 teaspoons salted butter, melted, divided
1 teaspoon light brown sugar
1 pineapple slice
1 maraschino cherry, stemmed
3 tablespoons all-purpose flour
1 tablespoon plus 1½ teaspoons granulated sugar
¼ teaspoon baking powder
⅟₁₆ teaspoon salt
¼ teaspoon vanilla extract
1 tablespoon plus 1½ teaspoons 2% milk

ALUMINUM FOIL IN THE AIR FRYER

Using aluminum foil to cover the cake in the air fryer will prevent the cake from overbrowning, but be careful, as the foil may blow off. Wrap the foil tightly around the container and stay close while the food is cooking. If the foil dislodges, you'll hear a crinkly noise and will have to reattach it.

1   Spray a ramekin with nonstick cooking spray.

2   Place ½ teaspoon butter in ramekin and sprinkle with brown sugar. Lay pineapple slice in ramekin and put cherry in center of pineapple.

3   In a medium bowl, mix flour, granulated sugar, baking powder, and salt.

4   In a small bowl, mix remaining 1½ teaspoons butter, vanilla, and milk. Add butter mixture to flour mixture and whisk until combined. To keep cake light, do not overmix.

5   Pour batter on top of pineapple. Place a small piece of aluminum foil over top of ramekin and crimp tightly around the edges.

6   Place ramekin in air fryer basket. Air fry at 350°F for 8 minutes. Open air fryer and remove foil. Air fry 7 minutes more.

7   Using pot holders, remove ramekin from air fryer. Then place a small plate on top of ramekin and flip ramekin to remove cake. Serve.

PER SERVING

CALORIES: 292 | **FAT:** 8g | **SODIUM:** 338mg | **CARBOHYDRATES:** 52g | **FIBER:** 1g | **SUGAR:** 32g | **PROTEIN:** 4g

Air Fryer–Grilled Peaches

Grilled peaches are a great summertime treat, but who wants to heat up the grill just for one peach? Now you can make grilled peaches in your air fryer! They're ready in minutes and just as delicious as the grilled version (even if your peaches aren't quite ripe). Use ice cream instead of whipped topping if you prefer.

Hands-On Time: 3 minutes
Cook Time: 10 minutes

Serves 1

- 1 medium yellow peach
- 2 tablespoons crushed graham cracker
- 2 tablespoons light brown sugar
- 1 tablespoon cold salted butter, cut into tiny cubes
- 2 tablespoons whipped topping

1 Cut a peach into 4 wedges and pull out the pit.

2 Line air fryer with parchment paper. Lay peach wedges skin-side up on parchment. Air fry at 350°F for 5 minutes.

3 In a small bowl, mix cracker crumbs, sugar, and butter.

4 Open air fryer and flip wedges skin-side down. Spoon crumb mixture on top of wedges, keeping butter on top as best you can. Air fry 5 minutes more.

5 Using a big spoon, spoon wedges onto a small plate and top with whipped topping. Spoon any excess topping mixture from parchment onto whipped topping. Serve.

PER SERVING

CALORIES: 323 | FAT: 13g | SODIUM: 146mg | CARBOHYDRATES: 51g | FIBER: 3g | SUGAR: 43g | PROTEIN: 2g

Blueberry Cobbler

Fruit cobblers are a super-simple dessert any time of year. Whether you're using fresh, frozen, or canned fruit, they all make a delicious cobbler. This cobbler is even more special because of the sugary crust on top. The first bite when you crack that crust is the best!

Hands-On Time: 10 minutes
Cook Time: 15 minutes

Serves 1

⅓ cup blueberries
1 tablespoon plus
   1½ teaspoons light brown sugar
1 tablespoon salted butter, softened
1⁄16 teaspoon salt
2 tablespoons all-purpose flour
⅛ teaspoon baking powder
2 tablespoons 2% milk
1 tablespoon granulated sugar
½ teaspoon cornstarch
1 teaspoon hot water

FRUITS TO USE IN COBBLER

This recipe calls for blueberries, but if you're not a fan, you can easily replace them with peaches, raspberries, blackberries, or mixed berries. Fresh or frozen fruit works best for this recipe.

1 Spray a ramekin with nonstick cooking spray. Pour blueberries into ramekin.

2 In a pint jar, using an electric hand mixer on medium speed, beat brown sugar and butter until creamed.

3 Add salt, flour, baking powder, and milk to jar. Beat until a batter forms. Pour batter over blueberries.

4 In a small bowl, mix granulated sugar and cornstarch. Sprinkle sugar mixture over top of batter in ramekin. Sprinkle water over sugar so all sugar is coated.

5 Cover ramekin with aluminum foil, tucking ends of foil under ramekin, then place in air fryer. Air fry at 375°F for 10 minutes.

6 Remove foil and air fry 5 minutes more.

7 Using pot holders, remove ramekin from air fryer and serve warm.

PER SERVING

CALORIES: 331 | **FAT:** 11g | **SODIUM:** 316mg | **CARBOHYDRATES:** 55g | **FIBER:** 2g | **SUGAR:** 38g | **PROTEIN:** 3g

Baked Apples with a Crumble Topping

Air fryer baked apples are delicious! They have all the best parts of an apple pie without all the calories and take no time to make. If you're worried about slicing through the apple halves, lay chopsticks on either side of the apple as a guide. Serve with whipped cream or vanilla ice cream.

Hands-On Time: 10 minutes
Cook Time: 16 minutes

Serves 1

- 1 medium Pink Lady apple
- 2 tablespoons salted butter, softened, divided
- 2 tablespoons granulated sugar, divided
- ½ tablespoon ground cinnamon
- 3 tablespoons old-fashioned rolled oats

APPLE VARIETIES

Many varieties of apples work well in this sweet and delicious recipe. If you can't find Pink Lady, other good apple choices are Jonagold, Honeycrisp, Braeburn, and Mutsu.

1 Peel apple and slice in half vertically. Carefully remove core, but do not break apple halves.

2 Place apple halves flat-side down on a cutting board and use a paring knife to make thin slices into the apple, not slicing completely through.

3 Line air fryer with parchment paper. Lay apple halves flat-side down on parchment. Brush apples with 1 tablespoon butter and sprinkle with 1 tablespoon sugar. Air fry at 375°F for 10 minutes.

4 Melt remaining tablespoon butter in the microwave in a medium microwave-safe bowl for 20 seconds. Add remaining tablespoon sugar, cinnamon, and oats to butter and stir.

5 Open air fryer and pat apples with oat mixture. Press mixture into open crevices in apples. Air fry 5 minutes more.

6 Remove apples from air fryer and remove parchment. Pour any sauce runoff onto apples. Serve.

PER SERVING

CALORIES: 462 | **FAT:** 23g | **SODIUM:** 183mg | **CARBOHYDRATES:** 62g | **FIBER:** 8g | **SUGAR:** 43g | **PROTEIN:** 3g

Chocolate Peanut Butter S'mores

S'mores aren't just a summertime campfire treat—you can make them in just 4 minutes, right in your air fryer. Note: You may need to use your phone's timer instead of a kitchen timer, as there are very short increments of time in this recipe.

Hands-On Time: 2 minutes
Cook Time: 2 minutes

Serves 1

2 graham cracker sheets
   (4 squares)
2 large marshmallows
2 peanut butter cups

1   Break graham crackers into 4 squares. Place 2 squares on air fryer tray, near walls of air fryer.

2   Top each square with 1 marshmallow. Add remaining 2 graham cracker squares on top, tilting each one down toward the wall of the air fryer at a 45° angle. This makes a little "house" out of graham crackers that will keep the marshmallow from blowing in the air fryer.

3   Air fry at 360°F for 1 minute 30 seconds.

4   Open air fryer and, using silicone tongs, delicately lift each top graham cracker and marshmallow. Place 1 peanut butter cup on each bottom cracker. Replace marshmallow and cracker "roof" over each peanut butter cup.

5   Air fry 15 seconds more.

6   Open air fryer and transfer s'mores to a small plate. Smush crackers together and serve!

PER SERVING

CALORIES: 396 | **FAT:** 16g | **SODIUM:** 299mg | **CARBOHYDRATES:** 58g | **FIBER:** 3g | **SUGAR:** 36g | **PROTEIN:** 7g

Chocolate Chip Doughnut Bread Pudding

Leftover glazed doughnuts come back to life when you make them into a single-serving bread pudding. The creamy custard is made even more delicious when you add chocolate chips to this doughnut mixture.

Hands-On Time: 5 minutes
Cook Time: 12 minutes

Serves 1

- 1 (1½-ounce) glazed doughnut, cut into ½" pieces
- 2 tablespoons semisweet chocolate chips
- 1 large egg
- ¼ cup 2% milk
- ½ teaspoon granulated sugar
- ½ teaspoon vanilla extract
- 1 teaspoon confectioners' sugar

1   Spray a ramekin with nonstick cooking spray. Place doughnut pieces and chocolate chips in ramekin.

2   In a small bowl, whisk together egg, milk, granulated sugar, and vanilla. Pour over doughnut and push doughnut into egg mixture. Cover and refrigerate 10 minutes.

3   Remove from refrigerator and place ramekin in air fryer. Air fry at 320°F for 10 minutes, until doughnut pieces are golden brown.

4   Using pot holders, remove ramekin from air fryer. Sprinkle bread pudding with confectioners' sugar and serve.

PER SERVING

CALORIES: 405 | FAT: 21g | SODIUM: 249mg | CARBOHYDRATES: 42g | FIBER: 2g | SUGAR: 17g | PROTEIN: 12g

CUSTOMIZE IT

If you're not in the mood for the traditional fillings of this recipe, you can replace it with any number of other add-ins to bread pudding! Here are some delicious ideas that will deliciously alter the recipe: white chocolate chips and crushed pistachios, peanut butter and chocolate chips, or peaches and blueberries!

Blueberry Muffins

This recipe is simple, delicious, and just enough to satisfy any sweet tooth.

Hands-On Time: 10 minutes
Cook Time: 14 minutes

Serves 1

1 large egg
¼ cup granulated sugar
¼ cup vegetable oil
⅛ teaspoon vanilla extract
½ cup all-purpose flour
¼ teaspoon baking powder
1⁄16 teaspoon salt
⅓ cup fresh blueberries

1   In a medium bowl, mix egg, sugar, oil, and vanilla. Add flour, baking powder, and salt and mix just until combined. Do not overmix. Fold in blueberries.

2   Spray three silicone baking cups with non-stick cooking spray. Pour batter into baking cups, then place cups in air fryer. Air fry at 350°F for 8 minutes. Lower temperature to 300°F and air fry 6 minutes more.

3   Let muffins rest 3–5 minutes in air fryer.

4   Remove baking cups from air fryer and turn upside down to remove muffins. Serve warm.

PER SERVING

CALORIES: 1,015 | FAT: 58g | SODIUM: 338mg | CARBOHYDRATES: 106g | FIBER: 3g | SUGAR: 55g | PROTEIN: 13g

Chocolate Hazelnut and Strawberry Fluffadilla

Fill your tortilla for a delicious, simple dessert in minutes.

Hands-On Time: 5 minutes
Cook Time: 3 minutes

Serves 1

1 (6") low-carb flour tortilla
2 tablespoons chocolate hazelnut spread
2 large marshmallows, halved
1 strawberry, sliced

1   Lay tortilla on a cutting board and spread chocolate hazelnut spread over entire tortilla. Place marshmallows over middle of tortilla. Place strawberry slices in between marshmallows.

2   Fold tortilla in half and press shut around edges.

3   Lightly spritz top of quesadilla with olive oil spray and place in air fryer. Air fry at 350°F for 3 minutes.

4   Using tongs, remove quesadilla and serve.

PER SERVING

CALORIES: 318 | FAT: 13g | SODIUM: 276mg | CARBOHYDRATES: 51g | FIBER: 11g | SUGAR: 29g | PROTEIN: 7g

Strawberry Zucchini Bread

Zucchini bread is delicious on its own, but adding fresh strawberries gives it an extra touch of sweetness. You'll be hard-pressed not to gobble this up in minutes, especially when it's warm from the air fryer. You could also substitute blueberries or raspberries for the strawberries.

Hands-On Time: 10 minutes
Cook Time: 22 minutes

Serves 1

1 large egg
¼ cup granulated sugar
2 tablespoons vegetable oil
¼ teaspoon vanilla extract
¼ cup plus 1 teaspoon all-purpose flour, divided
⅛ teaspoon baking soda
⅛ teaspoon baking powder
1 teaspoon ground cinnamon
¹⁄₁₆ teaspoon salt
⅓ cup grated zucchini
⅓ cup diced strawberries

1 In a small bowl, using an electric hand mixer on high speed, beat egg and sugar for 30 seconds. Add oil and vanilla and mix on high for 20 seconds. Add ¼ cup flour, baking soda, baking powder, cinnamon, and salt. Mix just until combined.

2 Sprinkle remaining 1 teaspoon flour over batter. Fold zucchini and strawberries into batter.

3 Spray a mini loaf pan with nonstick cooking spray. Pour batter into pan. Place pan in air fryer and air fry at 320°F for 22 minutes.

4 Open air fryer and, using pot holders, remove pan. Let cool 5 minutes.

5 Run a butter knife along sides of pan. Remove bread from pan. Serve warm.

PER SERVING

CALORIES: 666 | **FAT:** 32g | **SODIUM:** 436mg | **CARBOHYDRATES:** 84g | **FIBER:** 4g | **SUGAR:** 54g | **PROTEIN:** 11g

Chocolate Melting Cake

This Chocolate Melting Cake is a decadent, delicious option for special occasions or private movie nights in! Made in a ramekin, this chocolate cake has a melted center that is almost like pudding. With just five ingredients, it's simple too. Top it with whipped cream or get adventurous and add a dollop of peanut butter.

Hands-On Time: 7 minutes
Cook Time: 8 minutes

Serves 1

1½ ounces dark chocolate
3 tablespoons salted butter
1 large egg
1 tablespoon plus 1½ teaspoons granulated sugar
1 tablespoon plus 1½ teaspoons all-purpose flour

1   Spray a ramekin with nonstick cooking spray.

2   In a small microwave-safe dish, microwave chocolate and butter 30 seconds at a time until melted.

3   In a separate small bowl, whisk egg and sugar until combined. Add flour and mix for 1 minute. Fold chocolate mixture into flour mixture until combined.

4   Pour batter into ramekin. Add 1" water to bottom of air fryer. Place ramekin on tray above water in air fryer basket. If using oven-style air fryer, place pan with 1" water on lower rack and then place ramekin on rack above water. Air fry at 390°F for 7 minutes.

5   Using pot holders, remove ramekin from air fryer. Let cool 3 minutes.

6   Run a butter knife around edges of ramekin. Place a small plate on top of ramekin and flip ramekin to remove cake. Serve.

PER SERVING

CALORIES: 724 | FAT: 49g | SODIUM: 353mg | CARBOHYDRATES: 54g | FIBER: 3g | SUGAR: 39g | PROTEIN: 10g

Chocolate Chip Brookie

This Chocolate Chip Brookie will satisfy any sweet tooth. A thick chocolate chip cookie layer with brown sugar and vanilla, topped with a chewy chocolate brownie layer—this dessert is one to eat with a spoon and is best served with a big scoop of vanilla ice cream.

Hands-On Time: 15 minutes
Cook Time: 11 minutes

Serves 1

Cookie Layer

1 tablespoon salted butter, softened
1 tablespoon granulated sugar
2 teaspoons light brown sugar
1 tablespoon applesauce
⅛ teaspoon vanilla extract
3 tablespoons all-purpose flour
⅛ teaspoon baking powder
¹⁄₁₆ teaspoon salt
2 tablespoons semisweet chocolate chips

Brownie Layer

2 tablespoons granulated sugar
1 tablespoon salted butter, melted
1 tablespoon applesauce
1 tablespoon cocoa powder
1 tablespoon all-purpose flour
¹⁄₁₆ teaspoon baking powder
¹⁄₁₆ teaspoon salt

1 Spray a small baking dish or mini cast iron pan with nonstick cooking spray.

2 To make Cookie Layer: In a small bowl, using an electric hand mixer on medium speed, beat together butter, granulated sugar, brown sugar, applesauce, and vanilla until creamy. Add flour, baking powder, and salt and mix just until combined. Fold in chocolate chips.

3 To make Brownie Layer: In a separate small bowl, stir together sugar and butter. Add applesauce and stir. Add cocoa, flour, baking powder, and salt and stir until combined.

4 Spread cookie dough in bottom of dish. Pour brownie batter on top of cookie dough and spread to cover.

5 Place dish in air fryer and air fry at 350°F for 11 minutes. Let set in air fryer 3–5 minutes. After letting brookie rest, open and check with a toothpick in the center. The toothpick should come out fairly clean when done.

6 Using pot holders, remove dish from air fryer and serve warm.

PER SERVING

CALORIES: 635 | FAT: 29g | SODIUM: 567mg | CARBOHYDRATES: 94g | FIBER: 5g | SUGAR: 64g | PROTEIN: 6g

Caramelized Banana

Bananas have a light natural sweetness that is enhanced with just a touch of brown sugar and cinnamon. Top with ice cream and chopped nuts for an extra treat.

Hands-On Time: 5 minutes
Cook Time: 8 minutes

Serves 1

1 medium banana
2 tablespoons light brown sugar
1/16 teaspoon ground cinnamon

1 Leaving peel on, slice banana in half lengthwise.

2 Line air fryer basket with parchment paper. Place banana halves faceup in air fryer.

3 Coat each half with sugar and sprinkle with cinnamon. Air fry at 380°F for 8 minutes.

4 Remove bananas from air fryer and serve.

PER SERVING

CALORIES: 209 | **FAT:** 0g | **SODIUM:** 8mg | **CARBOHYDRATES:** 54g | **FIBER:** 3g | **SUGAR:** 41g | **PROTEIN:** 1g

Lemon Blueberry Cheater Pie

This is a cheater pie because there's no need for piecrust. Using bread instead of pie dough saves time and still gives it the texture of crust.

Hands-On Time: 5 minutes
Cook Time: 8 minutes

Serves 1

1 (¾"-thick) slice white bread
3½ ounces lemon pudding cup
1 tablespoon fresh blueberries
¼ teaspoon granulated sugar
1 large egg, beaten

1 Spray a ramekin with nonstick cooking spray.

2 Lay bread on cutting board. Using a rolling pin, flatten bread. Cut bread slice in half. Place half of bread slice in ramekin.

3 Spoon pudding into ramekin and top with blueberries. Place other half of bread slice on top and tuck into ramekin. Sprinkle sugar on top of bread. Using a pastry brush, lightly brush egg onto pie.

4 Place ramekin in air fryer and air fry at 340°F for 8 minutes.

5 Carefully remove ramekin with pot holders. Let pie cool 5 minutes before serving.

PER SERVING

CALORIES: 313 | **FAT:** 9g | **SODIUM:** 392mg | **CARBOHYDRATES:** 43g | **FIBER:** 1g | **SUGAR:** 21g | **PROTEIN:** 12g

Rhubarb Crisp

Rhubarb is one of the most delicious summertime vegetables. It's tart and sweet. You only need one stalk of rhubarb for this recipe, and you can use fresh or frozen. Serve with whipped cream or vanilla ice cream.

Hands-On Time: 10 minutes
Cook Time: 10 minutes

Serves 1

- **2 tablespoons granulated sugar**
- **1 teaspoon cornstarch**
- **½ cup diced rhubarb**
- **3 tablespoons old-fashioned rolled oats**
- **2 tablespoons light brown sugar**
- **2 tablespoons salted butter, melted**
- **1 tablespoon all-purpose flour**
- **¼ teaspoon ground cinnamon**

1 In a medium bowl, mix granulated sugar and cornstarch. Toss rhubarb (thawed, if using frozen) in sugar mixture. Spray a ramekin with nonstick cooking spray. Spoon rhubarb into ramekin.

2 Place ramekin in air fryer and air fry at 350°F for 5 minutes.

3 In a small bowl, combine oats, brown sugar, butter, flour, and cinnamon until mixture resembles coarse crumbs.

4 Open air fryer and sprinkle oat mixture over rhubarb. Air fry 5 minutes more.

5 Using pot holders, remove ramekin from air fryer and serve.

PER SERVING

CALORIES: 510 | FAT: 23g | SODIUM: 191mg | CARBOHYDRATES: 74g | FIBER: 3g | SUGAR: 53g | PROTEIN: 4g

FREEZING RHUBARB

Rhubarb is plentiful in May and June, but you should not use it fresh after July 4. If you have an excess of rhubarb before July 4, cut it into 1" chunks. Place chunks on a baking sheet and freeze 2 hours. Remove from baking sheet and place in zip-top freezer bags and freeze up to 1 year.

Strawberry Cheesecake Wrap

Strawberries and cream cheese pair perfectly together. Wrap them up in a low-carb tortilla shell and you've got a handheld dessert any night of the week. A touch of cinnamon and sugar at the end adds a bit of sweetness.

Hands-On Time: 5 minutes
Cook Time: 6 minutes

Serves 1

- 2 ounces full-fat cream cheese, softened
- 2 teaspoons confectioners' sugar
- 1 (6") low-carb flour tortilla
- 2 strawberries, diced
- 2 teaspoons salted butter, melted
- 1 tablespoon granulated sugar
- 1 teaspoon ground cinnamon

1 In a small bowl, mix cream cheese and confectioners' sugar. Spread cream cheese mixture on tortilla. Sprinkle strawberries on cream cheese. Fold sides of tortilla in and roll like a burrito.

2 Line air fryer with parchment paper. Place wrap on parchment and air fry at 300°F for 3 minutes.

3 Remove wrap from air fryer and roll in butter.

4 Mix granulated sugar and cinnamon. Sprinkle wrap on all sides with sugar mixture.

5 Return wrap to air fryer and air fry 3 minutes more.

6 Using tongs, carefully remove wrap from air fryer. Let cool 3 minutes before serving.

PER SERVING

CALORIES: 410 | **FAT:** 26g | **SODIUM:** 516mg | **CARBOHYDRATES:** 39g | **FIBER:** 11g | **SUGAR:** 21g | **PROTEIN:** 9g

US/Metric Conversion Chart

VOLUME CONVERSIONS

US Volume Measure	Metric Equivalent
⅛ teaspoon	0.5 milliliter
¼ teaspoon	1 milliliter
½ teaspoon	2 milliliters
1 teaspoon	5 milliliters
½ tablespoon	7 milliliters
1 tablespoon (3 teaspoons)	15 milliliters
2 tablespoons (1 fluid ounce)	30 milliliters
¼ cup (4 tablespoons)	60 milliliters
⅓ cup	90 milliliters
½ cup (4 fluid ounces)	125 milliliters
⅔ cup	160 milliliters
¾ cup (6 fluid ounces)	180 milliliters
1 cup (16 tablespoons)	250 milliliters
1 pint (2 cups)	500 milliliters
1 quart (4 cups)	1 liter (about)

WEIGHT CONVERSIONS

US Weight Measure	Metric Equivalent
½ ounce	15 grams
1 ounce	30 grams
2 ounces	60 grams
3 ounces	85 grams
¼ pound (4 ounces)	115 grams
½ pound (8 ounces)	225 grams
¾ pound (12 ounces)	340 grams
1 pound (16 ounces)	454 grams

OVEN TEMPERATURE CONVERSIONS

Degrees Fahrenheit	Degrees Celsius
200 degrees F	95 degrees C
250 degrees F	120 degrees C
275 degrees F	135 degrees C
300 degrees F	150 degrees C
325 degrees F	160 degrees C
350 degrees F	180 degrees C
375 degrees F	190 degrees C
400 degrees F	205 degrees C
425 degrees F	220 degrees C
450 degrees F	230 degrees C

BAKING PAN SIZES

American	Metric
8 x 1½ inch round baking pan	20 x 4 cm cake tin
9 x 1½ inch round baking pan	23 x 3.5 cm cake tin
11 x 7 x 1½ inch baking pan	28 x 18 x 4 cm baking tin
13 x 9 x 2 inch baking pan	30 x 20 x 5 cm baking tin
2 quart rectangular baking dish	30 x 20 x 3 cm baking tin
15 x 10 x 2 inch baking pan	30 x 25 x 2 cm baking tin (Swiss roll tin)
9 inch pie plate	22 x 4 or 23 x 4 cm pie plate
7 or 8 inch springform pan	18 or 20 cm springform or loose bottom cake tin
9 x 5 x 3 inch loaf pan	23 x 13 x 7 cm or 2 lb narrow loaf or pate tin
1½ quart casserole	1.5 liter casserole
2 quart casserole	2 liter casserole

Index

Note: Page numbers in **bold** indicate recipe category lists.

About the Author

Heather Johnson is a recipe developer, food stylist, food photographer, and TV contributor. She is the creator of *The Food Hussy*, a food and travel blog featuring quick and easy recipes that are great for every day and every occasion, including air fryer recipes and copycat restaurant recipes. She appeared in Season 30 of *Guy's Grocery Games* on Food Network. Heather has a passion for cooking, food, and travel. She lives in the Cincinnati area with her puppies, Mysty and Weiner, and kitties, Diggie and Maisy.

Quick, easy, & delicious recipes, using 5 INGREDIENTS or less!

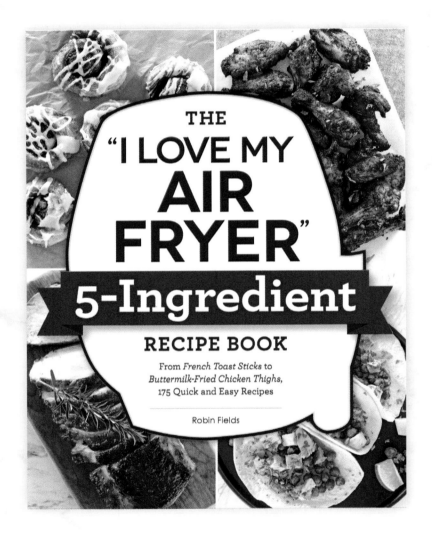

PICK UP OR DOWNLOAD YOUR COPY TODAY!